An Era of Addiction

An Era of Addiction

The Evolution of Dependency

W. L. Houser-Thomas

Writers Club Press
New York Lincoln Shanghai

An Era of Addiction
The Evolution of Dependency

Writers Club Press
an imprint of iUniverse, Inc.

For information address:
iUniverse, Inc.
2021 Pine Lake Road, Suite 100
Lincoln, NE 68512
www.iuniverse.com

ISBN: 0-595-25348-2 (pbk)
ISBN: 0-595-65112-7 (cloth)

Printed in the United States of America

This book is for my children, Adam, Olivia, and Jesse. Without them I might have never noticed that the future is a scary place.

"The immobility of our world is an illusion.
We spin. We speed through space.
We circle the sun. We live on a wandering star.
The apparent steadiness of the Earth lulls the mind into a false
stability.
The body's footing feels so secure that the mind naturally interprets
the daily bobbing up and down of the Sun, the moon, the planets,
and the stars as motions entirely external to the Earth."[1]

—*Galileo's Daughter*
Dava Sobel

Descriptive Introduction of the Silent Weapon

"Everything that is expected from an ordinary weapon is expected from a silent weapon by its creators, but only in its own manner of functioning.

It shoots situations, instead of bullets; propelled by data processing, instead of a chemical reaction (explosion); originating from bits of data, instead of gun powder; from a computer instead of gun; operated by a computer programmer, instead of a marksman; under the orders of a banking magnate, instead of a military general.

It makes no obvious explosive noises, causes no obvious physical or mental injuries, and does not obviously interfere with anyone's daily social life.

Yet it makes an unmistakable "noise," causes unmistakable physical and mental damage, and unmistakably interferes with daily social life, i.e., unmistakable to a trained observer, one who knows what to look for.

The public cannot comprehend this weapon, and therefore cannot believe that they are being attacked and subdued by a weapon.

The public might instinctively feel that something is wrong (ISN"T THAT THE TRUTH?), but because of the technical nature of the silent weapon, they cannot express their feeling in a rational way, or handle the problem with intelligence. Therefore, they do not know how to cry for help, and do not know how to associate with others to defend themselves against it.

When a silent weapon is applied gradually, the public adjusts/adapts to its presence and learns to tolerate its encroachment on their lives until the pressure (psychological via income) becomes too great and they crack up.

Therefore, the silent weapon is a type of biological warfare. It attacks the vitality, options, and mobility of the individuals of a society by knowing, understanding, manipulating, and attacking their sources of natural and social energy, and their physical, mental, and emotional strengths and weakness."[2]

Behold a Pale Horse
William Cooper

Contents

Part II   The Evolution of Dependency

Part III   The Power of Influence

Author's Note

*"Every since I was a little girl, I always wanted to be somebody.
Now I see I should have been more specific."*

—Lily Tomlin

An Era of Addiction is about belief systems, patterns of behavior, and addictive processes in the context of cultural transitions, eventual ramifications, and physical realities. It is an analysis encompassing a wide range of dependent patterns and their resulting consequences. It is about the residual of certain lifestyle dynamics that tend to be overlooked, ignored, or rationalized even though these particular dynamics are illogical and often destructive. No different than a puppet on a string, we are manipulated. The most powerful players behind this manipulation exist within the cracks of our world, they are the perpetrators of the ever ominous 'more;' the bits and pieces that are often lost in a rapid-fire culture, leaving a residual of pressure and stress. These subliminal feeds are sugarcoated with falsified generalities to hide their lethality. And, it is these exact dynamics, which will, without question, dictate evolution and survival, especially for our children and our children's children. If you question the severity of this reality just remember that one in three of us will die of cancer: A slow, lethal, physical implosion, the ultimate violation of our genetics, and terrorism at a cellular level. As John Ralston Saul states in *Voltaire's Bastards:*

*A civilization unable to differentiate between illusion and reality
is usually believed to be at the tail end of its existence.*

An Era of Addiction also asks and answers such questions as: What role does the infiltration of chemicals and pollutants play in this grand shift we are experiencing? Are our brains changed by the toxins in the environment? In our food? How do the hormones shot into cattle, pork, and chickens affect our bodies? Is this the reason why 59% of Americans are overweight? Why there is such a high degree of antibiotic resistant illness? Why do the United States and Canada account for a startling 95% of the world's Ritalin consumption?[3] Does the biotech industry create more than severe allergic reactions? Are we quietly being transformed, even brainwashed, into compliance by the complex residual of a re-structured body with the infiltration of this industrialized food? Bacteria laced water? A re-wired brain by the affects of commercialism via the media? Is our culture so mesmerized by fantasy that it lacks the ability to separate and internalize the consequences of certain realities? And, most importantly, this book clarifies the power addiction plays in the each of our lives concerning all of the fore-mentioned issues.

> *"If those in charge of our society—politicians, corporate executives, and owners of the press and television—can dominate our ideas, they will secure power. They will not need soldiers patrolling the streets. We will control ourselves."*
>
> —Howard Zinn

An Era of Addiction reveals the process that leads to and supports dependency at both individual and cultural levels. It shows what happens to a society that is built and continued on addictive patterns. Clear lines are present proving whom benefits from addiction and who gets trapped in its web. A materialistic culture that functions in a fog of unsubstantiated beliefs and data leaves permanent scars on the world and its people. With innocent people continuing to pay the price—be it terrorism, cancer, starvation, or hundreds of thousands of refugee families fleeing their country in fear of US missiles—with their lives. Walter Lippmann clearly reveals one unfortunate side: "The public must be put in place...so that each of us can live free of the trampling and the roar of the bewildered herd."

Nancy Snow also establishes in *Propaganda Inc:* "Democracy that Greek word for people-power, wasn't meant to be taken literally. Yes there would be elections. In between, however, democracy would be exercised by experts, through the proper channels, like national Security Counsels, Think Tanks and meetings in the halls of Congress." The system working within today's idea of progress insults intelligence, critical thought, and patriotism itself. To be discarded as a statistic—be it productivity, a pollster, or the popular Internet opinion, is to be dehumanized. And, where individualism is reduced to uniforms, constant analysis, name-tags, and the worship of a vicious clock-god there exists disturbed dominance, a dominance that needs our attention. As Peter Montague discusses:

> Sovereignty is in our hands, but the logic is the same: when people running a corporation assume rights and powers which the sovereign have not bestowed, or when they assault the sovereign people, this entity becomes an affront to the body politic. And like a cancer ravaging a human body, such a rebellious corporation must be cut out[4]…he corporate charter is granted by state legislatures. Without a charter a corporation ceases to exist.[5]

Without power-laden corporate fallout, the aggressiveness towards U.S. interests, those inside and outside the democracy, would be greatly decreased. Our children's future is at stake here. I want more for my children than jumping corporate hoops, responding to media engraved compulsions, or living in fear of random terrorist attacks. Balance is attainable; Sustainability is doable. If our children are to have any type of quality environment, freedom of thought, or opportunity the addictive nature of Western Culture must be reversed. If you picked this book up, you did it for a reason. Awareness is the first step towards any real change. The choice, the knowledge, and the awareness are lingering within your grasp. The power to change the world is, as it always has been, yours.

Acknowledgments

Thank You: The staff of Addiction's Research Center (ARC), especially Mary Glenn, who helps keep my life within reason from feeding us when I forget to cook, to helping me with my children, to making sure my vehicle has tags, and being the anchor for ARC. Also from ARC, I would like to thank Steve Shotts and Mike Rice who both make ARC look good, show up like clockwork and whose lectures provide wonderful efficiency. I would also like to thank those who have been enormously supportive in ideas and editing. They are Mike Rice; Maria McCarty; Michael Dabrowski; Mike Sprague; Linda K. Shoults-Underwood; and Warren Flint. **A very special thanks** to the wonderful writers of the world. The enormous amount of reading that aided in the writing of and provided the validation for this book could not have been done without the authors who continually fuel my knowledge as well as entertain me. I would like to especially thank Thom Hartmann. His book *The Last Hours' of Ancient Sunlight* was essential in waking me to the dynamics of the world. Mr. Hartmann's encouragement kept me going at a time when my projects seemed fruitless at best. Also, David Korten's *When Corporations Rule the World* and *The Post Corporate World* gave me details that reinforced what I had learned. These are amazing works and a must read for anyone concerned about the state of the world or their children's future.

Introduction:
Addiction and Belief

"Addiction is a pattern of behaviors that are continued even though they are recognizable by others, and perhaps even the perpetrator, that the pattern initiates negative results.

Addiction is a disease that has no boundaries, respect, or logic; an amazing, insidious, deceptive animal that stalks for the sake of the game, taking down individuals as well as nations regardless of social status, missile defense systems, or designer wear."

—W. L. Houser

Addiction is a story that's thousands of years old, creating false gods and worshipping idols of gold. We can see the malls as our Mecca and justify our rush of excitement in shopping or alcohol or Haagen Daz as an acceptable path to enlightenment. The proverbial elephant in the living room, the same mammal that roamed the mentality of Montezuma and danced on the barstools of Sodom and Gomorra, has found its oxygen tank on the streets of Western Culture. The best flashcard of this hold is the redressing of patriotism with consumerism; according to the Bush Administration terrorism can be fought by shopping. As Anna Quindlen writes in Newsweek, "If maxing out your plastic at the Gap is what patriotism has come to, then all the stealth bombers in the world can't save us from ourselves." [6]

Wavering between worldly comfort and spiritual enlightenment, trying not to be overwhelmed by the world but enjoy its simplicity, our lifestyles have become complex and fast paced. To insure the road to progress remains open, we demand a lot. Excess is an ongoing theme. Americans use up to 35% of the world's resources while representing less than 5% of the world's population. The average U.S. consumer throws out 1,500 pounds of trash each year. The United States has more malls than high schools; Americans spend more time shopping than reading. With the help of mass media and corporate influence consumption continues to spiral upwards with little attention to its fallout. Baselines have gone askew as progressive evolution is being reversed because addiction is hijacking the circuits involved in survival-based behavior. Bottom line, if you can derail survival circuitry with chemicals, you can do it with rewards too. And, as humans we like rewards with an army of readied suppliers.

To the brain a reward is a reward, regardless if it comes from chemicals or experience—be it cocaine, gambling, or shopping—if the pattern is pleasurable it is automatically reinforced in the brain and at some point is so wired into our response system that regardless of surrounding consequence the pattern becomes a compulsive part of our normal. This has been proven in research where the brains of cocaine addicts and gambling addicts are both wired to show where the brain is stimulated during cravings. The researchers had both sets of clients watch their particular nemesis on TV; cocaine addicts watched people snort coke, and gambling addicts watched gamblers. What the researchers found is that in both situations the same areas of the brains are active. Harvard University's Howard Shafferd says:

Addiction is the result of experience...repetitive, high emotion, high frequency experience.

Addiction rearranges our motivational priorities. Addiction relies on the very same neurobiological mechanisms that underlie learning and memory, with cravings predominantly being triggered by memories and situations, a powerful, dominant type of conditioning occurs. This conditioning is reinforced with our original wiring located in the limbic system—where impulse dominates. It is here that the infamous 'pleasure center' just waits for its moment. And, once that moment arrives, the cycle of addiction is in place resulting in the loss of various degrees of consciousness reinforced with the fore-mentioned wiring. According to the DSMIV-R:

> *Addictions, obsessions, compulsions—all are related to loss of voluntary control and getting trapped in repetitious, self-destructive behavior.*

This loss of conscious reason due to pleasure-based influence, which manipulate belief systems on a large scale within the boundaries of accepted patterns of a society is Cultural Addiction.

Addiction is not an impairment of intelligence; it is an impairment of thought that cannot see beyond instant gratification. It is an influence whose agenda takes precedence over its victim's higher aspirations. Beliefs pattern life after itself as brain chemistry automatically seeks to re-establish or protect its pleasure-centered positioning continually feeding status quo. Maintaining status quo is fine, unless the comfort level of a particular status creates harmful consequences. Addiction impairs our life because it dictates behaviors feeding self-destruction. The irony lying at the heart of Cultural Addiction is basically that as we believe ourselves to be self-sustaining if not progressive, we are slowly but surely killing ourselves. This conflict between belief, behavior, and reality creates overt and covert physical and emotional upheavals, which then seek relief, initiating the subtle cycle of addiction again.

The very fabric of society is woven with beliefs and the systems they create. These are powerful as they build normalcy by influencing our behaviors. It is our belief systems, whether we realize it or not, that determine how our daily lives unfold even if addictive patterns have been woven into them. Joseph Chilton Pearce estimates that 95% of all learning takes place below our awareness. This subliminal authority occurs more often than we realize with most beliefs built before we know it on what others have told us, on environmental feeds, and within generational baselines. These beliefs can to be loaded with propaganda, invalid rhetoric, and fear initiating influence that may only seek to control. The goal of control explains the dependent nature bred into globalization, industrialization, and the corporatization of not only America but of the world, which has resulted in vast economic and physical injustice as well as lethal environmental degradation. Thus, it is always essential to question who exactly is designing the pattern, structuring informational inputs and building mass belief systems. But how often do we ask these vital questions?

As Americans we automatically believe our country can protect us, but how can it protect us from our own excess? Excess that is fed via the media around the world, flaunted like the forbidden fruit to many, which then initiates other avenues of threat aside from the core nature of the addiction itself. But people don't like to look at their addictions, nor do they like their belief systems questioned—that is, until their world begins to disintegrate under the pressure of explosion after explosion before their very eyes. Then, and usually only then, do addicts ask for input on why their world is crumbling; on why everyone hates them. A question that has finally surfaced in the U.S. and a question that needs addressed with not only education, but the evaluation of beliefs and lifestyle patterns.

Ultimately it is evolution, which dictates survival. Being better than each other is the dance, with the most severe struggle being with those who need the same resources; however, isn't it important to look at the whole picture? Question who the competition is? Ask what might happen when the tables are turned? And, very importantly, wonder with whom you are competing? If you take the time and look in the mirror, you may realize the dilemma of building an empire on the backs of others. Yet survival rationalized competition seems to be the heartbeat of today's definition of progress. Competition driven motivation is the crux of many different stimuli. This stimulus is the concrete occurrence that provokes behavior. Most sought out stimulus ignites a 'feel good' sensation. (Though 'feeling good' may mean 'not feeling bad.') And, without motivation we would have failed to evolve.

But, there is a place where a line is crossed in which competition falls away, then motivation is driven by addiction. Addiction's core energy involves an attempt to fill this void; a sense of void that has been created by mass manipulators. The workings of addictive patterns in society are obviously a massive energy. It involves motivations, triggers, processes, and consequences. From the manipulation of the deal, to the reasons the addict falls prey, to the experience of consequences addicts live on the playground of compulsion and the 21st Century version of American Dream thrives on it.

"Reason is a narrow system
Swollen into ideology
With time and power it has become a dogma
Devoid of direction and disguised as disinterested inquiry
Like most religions, reason presents itself as the solution to the
problems it has created."

—John Ralston Saul
Voltaire's Bastards

PART I

Addictive Progression

o o o o o o o o o o o o o o o o o o o o o o o o o o o o o

"Reality serves up to us all our meaning
Who knows which myth to believe?
Who knows the facts or where they will lead us?
…We fashion out illusions in many ways.
We dress up in a car as if putting on a nice hat.
We sit in boxes all day, pretending the walls talk.
We weave daydreams, play lotteries, and plunge each evening
into the TV screen.
It takes us floating into a world of illusory concerns and
escapist fantasy
…All the things that control the mind—books, magazines,
letters, placards, posters, email,
Faxes, data—all the things that tell us what to think are all a
part of our world of fantasy.
They are today's religion.
Where do we go for salvation?"

—*The Physics of Consciousness*, *Evan Harris Walker*

1

Setting the Stage: A Modern Enchantment

"Nothing is more powerful than an idea whose time has come."
—Victor Hugo

"In my area of specialized retail I am somewhat of a hero. I give my customers what they want and should they happen to be a bit low on cash, I offer most of them loan plans. As part of the new economy, I only meet a supply-demand criterion. I am simply a business owner of a new breed; an entrepreneur of sorts who benefits from the lucrative business of dependency. This works for not only my family, but also my many associates. We are part of an elite group who betters our lives by capitalizing on the American Dream.

I am the way of progress. If I am to make it in this world I have to take advantage of the opportunities that are placed before me. If people end up addicted to the heroin I supply or the occasional crack-cocaine that falls into my inventory, it's their choice. We only supply the introductory offer for free, which is common practice and not enough to be held accountable in regards to our customers' future decisions.

So what if my prosperity is due to the weakness of others. Intimidation is the way of the world. It's evolution, survival of the fittest. So I may not have been born the fittest, with the most money or best education, but I have learned. I have created an arena where I am the fittest. I am simply Darwinism 21st Century style. I am cool. My ethics are reasonable if not admirable within my circle of peers. If you 'do gooders' would get off our backs with all your moralistic rhetoric; evolution

3

would play out, addicts would die off, and this whole overpopulation deal would ease up." Everyone in our court-ordered men's group, which included some pretty tough characters, cringed as Ray finished introducing himself.

Though Ray seems to have a decidedly more ruthless edge than most, his capitalizing on the existing human predisposition towards dependency is common practice and a marketer's dream. Without question, we are born dependent; and of all the species in existence, we need the most coddling. We are weaned from our mothers only to be nursed by a multitude of suppliers with no awareness of the transition. We are conditioned before we realize it; our lives built image by image, bit by bit towards specific patterns. Entertained or anesthetized? There is a fine line.

DATA AND DEPENDENCY

It is said that fifteen trillion bits of data come at the brain in an average lifetime. We are hit with a smorgasbord of incoming information driven by seen and unseen forces. Our brain either attempts to block the data or process it into information; however, certain data affects us subliminally getting processed in the arena of instinct without our conscious consent. The data that gets processed—be it conscious or subliminal—often decides our fate. If instinct dominates, then the data of instinct is all that is adhered to. And, a very important detail that shouldn't be overlooked, addiction dominates instinct.

No longer is addiction something that is someone else's problem, lingering behind doorways or around dark corners. No longer are the dealers of the world only doing business on street corners and in abandoned warehouses. They are in high rises and elaborate facilities. They are in malls making you perfect and on TV growing hamburgers in hamburger patches. They are on billboards with great smiles and commercials with the best deal. They are in our schools, on the radio, in print, and always taking residence in our psyche. They are an accepted participant, if not perpetrator, of how lives unfold daily. Our comfort often teeters on their decisions; their decisions always hinge on profitability. The strings of life are theirs to pull. They have us by the throat without our consent. No different than the coke freak, heroin junky, or alcoholic, dependency is a main part of our daily lives with denial coloring perception and excessive consumption being presented as normal.

Emotionally we are dependent on the media for entertainment, on pills to alleviate depression and caffeine to get us through the day. Economically we are dependent on big business, a system consisting of hierarchies once removed from empathy, who have no remorse in downsizing, using slave labor, creating pollution, fueling corruption, and leaving destruction in the wake of a vague definition of progress. We depend on the utility industry to keep our lives turned on and in sync, on cars to keep us going while the specific make or model bolsters our self-esteem. We no longer know how to feed or clothe ourselves, depending on outside sources for our most basic needs. Ill-will grows as foreign and state policy are manipulated to meet the needs of various corporate interests over the needs and best interests of the people.

As lifestyles continue to call for increased consumption there is a part of us that senses more to this story of excess than what we read on those billboards, advertisements, and hear on commercials. We watch the landscape of America changing; we also experience its loss of opportunity. McDonalds, being an icon for not only influence on other countries but American abundance, is one reflection of this shift. In 1968 McDonalds operated about 1000 restaurants, today it has 28,000 restaurants worldwide and opens approximately 2000 new ones each year.

McDonalds annually hires 1,000,000 people, more than any other American organization, public or private.[7] And importantly, McDonalds, though only one instigator, is proof of the corporate takeover of America, which ultimately materializes in that fact that 1% of the people in the United States own 80% of its property and 90% of its wealth. Aside from dietary indignities, those golden arches feed an imbalance that is threatening as it controls policy, dictates legislature, and wields its global sword. Where once many had some experience in farming and growing our own food, we now seek employment. It is now estimated that one out of every eight workers in America has at some point been employed by a McDonalds facility; no longer do our children plant seeds, they flip burgers.

SYSTEMATIC POWERLESSNESS

Some people openly acknowledge a sense of powerlessness, an awareness of the chronic imbalance in the world, a loss of faith in our government, a disdain and intolerance for ruling corporate biased agendas, a concern for people starving in other countries, as well as fears of cancer, random violence, pollution, and nuclear war. Yet, just like addicts who admit their nemesis, Western Culture continues to support these issues by default, feeding status quo, leaving an undeniable trail in the wake of consumption. Be it the production of massive amounts of meat in immoral conditions to feed such entities as McDonalds, the damaged lives left after a drunken rampage, corporate poisoning, the purchasing of products produced with slave labor, the ignoring of governmental imbalance, or individual apathy, a series of rationalizations occur to accommodate and protect cultural patterns.

The line between 'need' and 'want' continues to grow more and more vague with each commercial. Corporate offensiveness is fogged over by blizzards of propaganda. Wal-mart has more employees than the U.S. Post Office. Microsoft lobbies that it is not a monopoly. Enron executives sit with stashed billions while their workers are left destitute. We buy from corporations who lay off hundreds of thousands of people each month; somehow rationalizing it can't happen to us. Many navigate their lives with little savings, quickly giving away their hard-earned monies for a variety of media induced agenda's. Ultimately, we face stress, especially financial stress as we handover our paychecks. We not only give up personal power, but give power to big business in the form of cold, hard cash.

We are appeased by $300 or $500 tax rebates while the wealthy buy million dollar yachts with the new income generated from this political charade. Did we question the cuts needed to create these rebates? Do many of us realize that we may well end up putting out much, much more due to the fallout that will evolve from the environmental protection programs that were slashed to fund these rebates? How is it justified to spend this rebate at the nearest mass retailer? Do we ask ourselves if the purchase is somehow counter-productive? This 'instant-spend' thinking places most people back at the mercy of day-to-day drudgery to try and stay financially afloat.

Commercialism feeds materialistic thinking, which then feeds the power of presentation. Presentation provides that industrialization is the magic wand that makes everyone's world more accommodating, and that we are protected. But there is a price: we are afraid. Fear arrives from two venues: a fear of having less than, and fear from retaliatory avenues because we have more.

Having less than dictates an air of scarcity thinking; its deeper fear-based energy affecting core belief systems, which then subtly dominates lives as it determines habits. There exists a fear of losing what we have and of not having what we want. There is a fear of not having as much money as those we deem our competition have and fears surrounding looking less than those around us. We worry about everything from losing our jobs to losing our butts in the stock market to losing that last 10 pounds. We worry that the Jones' are winning.

Yet, the greatest fears stem from the threat of global annihilation in some form. Allowing inequality and starvation to enrage other countries less fortunate, supporting corrupt, corporate hierarchies and their ravages of other countries, and piecing together a miracle laser-type surveillance system in the name of protection all seems so much more complicated than sharing, living more simply, and boycotting the corporations that instigate many of the global nightmares we are facing.

But we are busy, continually moving towards unfulfilling activities as clear thought takes a back seat to instant gratification. As we build the illusion of security, having 'less than' has become an image that undermines any sense of stability initiating a search for more to appease discomfort. It seems we self-medicate as a national past time. For all types of addiction the common thread is seeking something outside the self for some type of emotional mitigation; thus when one continually medicates emotions, using some activity or substance to regularly alter their emotional state, they are indeed a type of addict.

"…My drug of choice is more."

—Robert Downing Jr.

2

Worldly Comfort

"Temptation will destroy our lives."

—Sara McLachlan

Tutter is one of my nephew's favorite characters on the television show "The Bear in the Big Blue House." Tutter is an easily excited, overwhelmed mouse who worries about things like running out of cheese. He then stocks up and when cheese is everywhere, he freaks out and worries about where to put all his cheese. Knee deep in cheese he obsesses on his dilemma. Without Bear, who calms him down, he would probably drink, which is never a good thing for a puppet. Tutter's thinking is always a bit left of center. He doesn't play pretend because he can't see himself as anyone else. He has this high-pitched, animated voice and scurries around in what I can only call an obsessive-compulsive delirium. Little monsters in his mind create much of Tutter's chaos; yet he can't see this. He is too busy preparing for a vague, self-created apocalypse.

PRESSURE OR PURPOSE?

Our lifestyles, like Tutter's, tend to push us around. But pressure and stress aren't generally goals for which we strive. We say we want peace and relaxation, yet continue to drudge forward. What influences us to push so hard? To always want more? What are we afraid we might miss? The good life? The flash of excitement? The latest trend? What is it we value as Americans? Our constitution states that we advocate equality, independence, and freedom, but do we see this reality materialize in the midst of such pressure? A basic premise our country is founded upon is freedom of religion. Yet even spirituality seems to have split off from dominant religious dogma and cultural trends.

Besieged with the idea that peace can be found in day-trading, cruising scenic wilderness spots in an SUV, or drinking the best beer, a severe confusion of circumstance breeds. Faith is lost to impulse. Like financial investment, emotional investment demands instant gratification. Divorce rates soar, family discord increases as serenity remains ominous. The feelings of loss, emptiness, and disconnectedness are common. There is a void beating at the heart of a culture that is manipulated by fear, feeds on scarcity, and has difficulty seeing beyond whatever golden calf that dominates focus. This consumeristic road to the Promised Land dead-ends in mental illness.

In the October issue of The New York Observer writer Jim Windolf asked: "Is everybody crazy? Americans are supposedly ailing at all time highs: 10 million suffer from seasonal affective disorder; 14 million are alcoholic; 15 million are pathologically socially anxious; 15 million are depressed; 3 million suffer panic attacks; 10 million have Borderline Personality Disorder; 5 million are obsessive-compulsive; 2 million are manic-depressive; 10 million are addicted to sex. All together this approximately adds up to 77% of the adult population being a total mess."[8] It seems that Tutter is not the only one with monsters.

Is it possible to find the communal cause of these ailments? Can sanity and peace be bought in a pill? Or an industrial size savings of cheese? Can tranquillity be found by simply putting aside the cravings and toys of our era and attempting to focus? Could addiction play a role swaying individuals, groups, and even cultural trends?

THE CLASSIC ADDICT

Jack is the classic addict. His addiction is about wanting more in a manner that is pathological. Jack smokes crack-cocaine and is able to afford large quantities of crack because of his system, his personalized idea of the American Dream. Jack gets huge commissions from the top-of-the-line homes he sells; buys cocaine; then sells it, tripling his commission. The bigger the deal, the better the commission; the more coke he can invest in and recycle, the more crack he can buy, then of course smoke. He's proud of his dream, even though the last bit—spending all of his profit—causes his system to fail. Yet Jack continually explained to our men's group, which included Ray as one of his supporters, how he would make a million dollars with his system. However, this would have to be after his court-ordered six-month-long stay in treatment with us.

Jack remained very positive about his lengthy stay in treatment. He could see that he needed to stop smoking crack. He could see how his continued use would simply cause more bad things to happen to him. He could see the obvious fallacy of his addiction. Unfortunately he had difficulty focusing on treatment. He was always calling his office for messages. His office was always calling with emergency after emergency. He continually missed the point about how all this chaos was a distraction, thus undermining the ability to see what was going so fatally wrong in his life.

After two weeks, the day bandages were to be removed from his hands, (when he came to treatment his hands were wrapped in bandages due to second degree burns because he had held the crack pipe too long over and over again) he informed our group that time was of the essence, he had a business that was calling for his attention and he needed to make more money. Amidst a chorus of concern from his fellow addicts, Jack left treatment still believing in a million-dollar strategy that would eventually kill him.

ALWAYS MORE

In nearly every conversation that I have with friends or acquaintances, they mention the need for more money. On one occasion, after hearing this scarcity dilemma from everyone around me for several days, I decided to ask one couple the dynamics of their need for more; what would be enough? As we sat in their $300,000 waterfront home the wife commented that $1,000,000 is what she wanted. I asked if they were in over their heads with such a nice house, the boat, and the vehicles. They said not at all. The mortgage on the house was a third of its value, and they were virtually debt free. The husband relayed that he solicits almost $100 an hour for his time while his wife brings in $70,000 a year. They also stated having what they felt to be sufficient savings for retirement. I told them I didn't understand their dilemma. They told me that they didn't understand my confusion.

I doubt that $1,000,000 would quench their thirst for more. Like Jack, the issue runs deeper, the longing for 'more' insatiable. History has shown that when this scarcity is present all patterns are derived from a fear-based stance. This fear-based energy is why there is such a huge degree of oppression, upheaval, and violence historically; aside from man's insatiable ego, there have always been obvious, violent pursuits for more.

Columbus is credited for discovering America yet he and his men were simply seeking more and more gold while leaving destruction and atrocity in their wake. The end result was the Haitian people's extinction. He also found the aboriginal tribe called the Tainos. He noted what a happy people they were—that was right before he slaughtered them all. Yet we now celebrate his life as a national holiday.

Presidents Andrew Jackson and Martin Van Buren were trying to acquire more and more land. As they marched thousands of Indians across the country they left the Trail of Tears in their wake. Ultimately the reservation idea is a bad one; segregation of any nature only leads to more and more fragmentation. And where there is fragmentation there is confusion, fear, and addiction.

General Custer sought more and more glory, and we know how that ended. Industrialization creates goods in larger and larger quantities yet quality took a dive, pollution soared and now we must buy our water in bottles. With help, we have grown to accept this as our 'normal.' Industrialization has undeniably created a degree of dependency to which no other time in human history can be remotely compared to.

Elvis kept taking more pills trying to survive circumstances that were more than he had bargained for, but the King died. Elvis seemed to be immobilized by unseen fears; he grappled with ghosts that only he could sense. Columbus was afraid of the Queen of Spain and drank too much. The Trail of Tears reflected a continual fear of the Indians. Custer needed more glory to feel alive, his ego urging him to new heights and greater risks. Industrialization is a reflection of man's highest goal to be better, but also gives free reign to the ramifications of human greed.

Ultimately, all these players had an addiction to 'more' and all experienced the corresponding consequences, which were unforeseen. Their definition of survival appears to have been made with an 'at-all-costs' baseline. Be it at the individual level or the cultural level, destructive excess happens infinitely more often than many are able to see.

CULTURAL DEMISE

Columbus, Elvis, and Custer were all considered to be of the elite, the best of the best per se. Throughout history, 'elite' cultures have intruded upon other cultures, and usually by force. These elite cultures then became parasites not only destroying the native cultures, but in time destroying themselves too. Self-destruction was not on their agenda; however, self-destruction was the outcome. Time after time great governments brought about their own demise by destroying the lands that fed them.

The early Sumerians were wiped out as a result of the extreme destruction of natural resources. The Sumerian kings maintained the cutting down of forests that took Lebanon from 90% forests to 7% forests in just 1,500 years. This in turn led to a reduction in downwind rainfall of 80%. At the same time, Mesopotamia was becoming overpopulated due to two major factors: the continual conquering of neighboring lands so they could cut their trees and the natural consequence of changing from a nomadic to a communal lifestyle.

In order to feed the expanding population, the continual planting and harvesting of barley exhausted the poorly irrigated land. The end result was the once lush, green land of Lebanon was turned into a desert. And, it remains that way today. This destruction caused the extinction of the Sumerian civilization.[9] The Greeks followed the Sumerians whose fate held the same results. The Romans then followed the Greeks—the same mistakes, the same fate. These were amazing empires collapsing mainly under the weight of their appetite and ignorance. Every major civilization of the last 7,000 years has ultimately self-destructed because of a shortage in their primary fuel supply due to deforestation, destruction of its watershed, and resulting soil depletion. And, the cycle is getting shorter. The Sumerians self-destructed in 4,000 years; the Greeks took 1,400 years; the Romans 1,100 years. Now we are on the same playground at our infant age of 225 years.

As Mark Horkheimer and Theodor Adorno state "Under existing conditions, the gifts of fortune themselves become elements of misfortune…Progress becomes regression." At the present rate of consumption, our craving for wood will strip the U.S. completely bare of all its forests in 50 years. Our oil reserves will last maybe 40 more years. Our food craving (with its extreme waste) has used up 75% of our topsoil.[10] Globally, as of 1998, fifteen hundred acres of land become desert each hour. Seventy-two acres of rain forest are destroyed each minute. A lot of this destruction is done by impoverished, desperate people trying to survive by creating grazing land to grow beef for the U.S.[11]

At the same time agri-business dumps 500 million pounds of herbicides into the water each year.[12] Nationally, industry pollutes air and water with 9 billion pounds of toxins a year, about 35 pounds per person. In one neat bundle these poisons include lead, PCBs, dioxin, and mercury,[13] which are all lethal to human evolution and survival. But, wood, water and food are big business; thus, this version of the American Dream marches on.

◆　　◆　　◆

Addicts continue to take without giving back, doing whatever they need to satisfy cravings. Industry races for new methods towards more products, manipulating whatever they need to as the ideals of success. Taking without giving back, industry puts more and more pressure on all that is life giving. Competition is rationalized as survival; tripping over the bones of rivals is considered par for the course. Boundaries are always being pushed further and further in the name of progress. New methods to meet cravings reduce the time-line on destruction.

Addiction feeds on itself, always gaining speed and ground. The first client I had was a 64-year-old alcoholic with cirrhosis of the liver and 45 years of drinking under his belt; he got sober. The last client I saw was a 24-year-old named Sara. She was a crack addict. Sara had been using crack for four months. Her dealer/boyfriend supplied her well. However, he supplied her more than he meant to.

One night, after she had attended a NA (Narcotics Anonymous) meeting, her heart exploded as she smoked up his hidden stash. Sara's four-year-old daughter dialed 911 when she found her mom 'sleeping' on the bathroom floor. As Antonio Machado says, "We build the road as we travel." Addiction, be it individual or cultural, is demise by one's own hand.

"Sometimes, no matter how hard you try, you can't escape the obvious.
But I think 'the obvious' is different for everyone.

My obvious just happened to be slits on my wrist, going the right way (vertically). I can't remember
wanting to die. Actually I can't remember cutting my wrists.
Before I always intentionally had cut them the wrong way, you know horizontally,
to manipulate whomever. This time I tried the right way.
Slitting my wrists the right way was my obvious. Some part of me had lost hope.
That was my obvious."

—Anonymous, she stayed clean about 6 months then overdosed
on vodka and pills.
It was considered accidental.

3

Communal Potential

"Nature has a funny way of breaking what does not bend."

—Jewel

On May 7, 2001 Newsweek reported, "14 million people in the United States are alcoholic or abuse alcohol. They are skid row bums and lace-curtain drunks, senseless rebels and charming rogues. They chill Louis Roederer Cristal champagne in silver buckets and swill Budweiser from plastic cups. They tell themselves they are not alcoholics because they don't drink before 5 p.m., or because they make it to work every day, or because dinner is always on the table on time.

But their excuses can't overcome the damage they do. Inga fell down a flight of stairs with her infant in her arms. Mark had five wives and five divorces. Betty polished off a pint of vodka, then carpooled fourth graders from soccer practice. Jeffrey committed strong-armed robbery. April, once shy, took off her clothes and danced for money. Martha threatened her husband with a carving knife…For active alcoholics drinking trumps reason. It distorts judgment. It severs the connection between behavior and consequence. It lays waste to marriages, friendships, and careers. It leaves children stranded. For alcoholics, love and logic can't hold a candle to liquor."[14]

THE PLEASURE CENTER

Productivity is god, dictating financial wellness, which in turn is supposed to secure survival and equate the 20th Century definition of success. These series of events naturally then wake the pleasure center of our brains. It is this pleasure center that is served when we win, feel powerful, get promoted, or get paid. It is this pleasure center that is accommodated when addicts feed it with every drink, joint, rock, or needle. Serving the pleasure center isn't addiction, as I have said, until the pattern that causes harm is continued even in light of consequences.

Everyone is born with this impulse towards instant gratification. Every brain is wired to remember pleasure as well as impulsively seek it out first and foremost. Addiction lives in the valleys of the most primitive area of our brains, in the nucleus accumbens as part of the limbic system where impulse dominates, overriding the reason of a less experienced frontal cortex. Without clear reason, perception can become distorted. Because of this distortion any addiction is no less devastating than daily doses of IV heroin or rock-cocaine. For it is not the drug of choice that is in question here, it is the issue of symptom versus problem.

When looking at addiction, the core problem, the cornerstone of all devastation, is the loss of conscious choice. The drunk driver doesn't consciously choose to kill, just as the wasteful consumer doesn't intentionally set out to pollute. Both situations are harmful and without intent. Yet these issues, though concern should be levied, are still not the epitome of the core threat. The essence of addiction, at a cultural level, threatens the very foundation upon which America was founded—freedom.

Where conscious decision making recedes so does freedom; the loss of freedom in any form, especially freedom of thought, is the main building block for such historic unfortunates as Caesar's Rome, Hitler's Germany or Stalin's Russia. Just as Hitler premised his policy as building the master race, detonating a power surge in his countrymen, often the roles we fall into are based on false premise. Images, goals, and lifestyles deemed as important are colored in such a way as to lead us to believe that we are living out the American Dream or the Essence of Life. But perhaps, just maybe, these endeavors are more akin to the Final Solution.

THE AMERICAN DREAM

The American Dream seems like a good thing, incorporating the expensive car, the big house, and a manicured persona. But, there are a lot of 'shoulds' in this dream. When dissected, the dream proves to be more about a belief system based on entrapment than one based on fulfillment. The American Dream has evolved from a pursuit of independence by hard work to the pursuit of things via the quickest and easiest manner available.

Often within this dream the loss of conscious choice is colored in such a way that it is deceiving, becoming the ultimate paradox. As we are bombarded with choice, often asking ourselves: which road should we take? What product should we buy? How much do I want to spend? Do I really want that Whopper? Similar to the addict, we rarely realize that it is in our best interest to walk away and steer clear of seductive playgrounds because it is on these playgrounds where lifestyle choices graduate from questionable 'wants' to uncontrollable 'needs.'

Keeping up, especially keeping up in style gets big applause as the list of 'needs' grows. The ability to perform well is worn as a badge of honor. But as many are busy competing, trying to survive or maybe even accomplishing a win, the ante is upped, then upped some more, and then 'need' expands its acreage. The race is next reported to be longer, the hills higher, and the water breaks more infrequent. Overwhelmed, trying to keep up, many forget that they don't have to stay on this playground. But then the memo comes stating that the wardrobe is outdated, the house is not big enough, and the car is too old. Victims begin to surface. Floating face down, these are the faceless sacrifices of success.

◆   ◆   ◆

On Aug 30, 1999, CNN reported that over the past four years the average blue-collar American worker's income has risen approximately 27% while the income of the typical corporate executive has risen approximately 483%. If the illusion of 'need' was not fed, if many were less dependent, a massive boycott of these inflated salaries could have been a voice of adjustment and sanity. CNN later reported a soaring stock market due to the lay off of 160,000 workers. The rationalization that this lay off is good because it shows that a booming economy is slowing seems a bit asinine. The push for better, faster production sets up workers to meet the mechanical expectations of greed. As the news makes statements such as 'workers are churning out goods and services at a more productive rate' workers are dehumanized. This mindless redemption—that of a protective hierarchy sustained by corporate power—is one of betrayal. Yet, it's through our own dependency on these corporations that we betray ourselves, as we remain lost in vicious repetition. Like Inga, Mark, Betty, Jeffrey, Martha, and April we are unable to see how threatening our cycles have become.

PROGRESSION THROUGH CYCLING

Threatening cycles—such as the process found in addiction—are simple. The cycle in addiction involves: seeking mood altering substances; then engaging in a mood-altering pattern; then recovering from use; and then planning the next use. This cycle reveals how the loss of analytical thought, preceding most sober decisions, happens. For addicts, as internal and external events fall out of their circle of control, without conscious consent, they are anesthetized by this pattern; they are hostages to a loss of control they can't see. Like Jack, Sara, and the others they unknowingly are clearing their own road to hell.

The Basic Cycle of Addiction

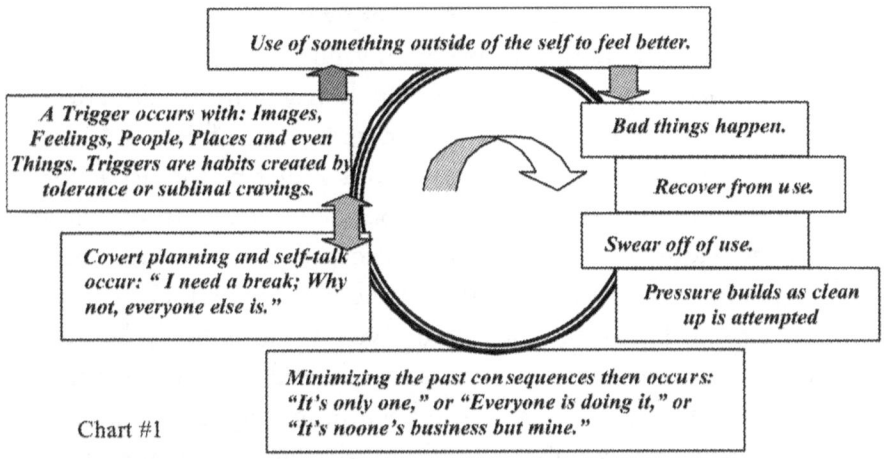

Use of something outside of the self to feel better.

A Trigger occurs with: Images, Feelings, People, Places and even Things. Triggers are habits created by tolerance or sublinal cravings.

Bad things happen.

Recover from use.

Swear off of use.

Covert planning and self-talk occur: " I need a break; Why not, everyone else is."

Pressure builds as clean up is attempted

Minimizing the past consequences then occurs: "It's only one," or "Everyone is doing it," or "It's noone's business but mine."

Chart #1

Addiction's cycle is also progressive as shown below by The Progression Line. This line reflects how social use turns into abuse as specific consequences arise. Then it shows how abuse turns into early stage addiction with escalating consequences. Finally the dominance of addiction, becoming the primary focus, takes over with more severe, often life threatening consequences.

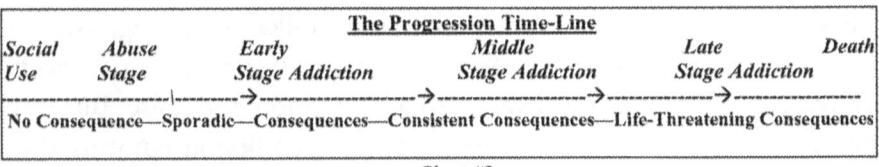

The Progression Time-Line					
Social Use	Abuse Stage	Early Stage Addiction	Middle Stage Addiction	Late Stage Addiction	Death

No Consequence—Sporadic—Consequences—Consistent Consequences—Life-Threatening Consequences

Chart #2

This progression is subtle, which is why it catches many people off guard. At first the pattern is fun, next it is stressful, then the next thing you know the pattern owns you and addiction is in place. At this point the addict is virtually incapable of awareness. While there is a progression of these patterns and their consequences there is also a continual manifestation of disabling denial. Denial keeps the addict unable to recognize their resident troubles due to a medicated psyche. This creates an inability for the addict to respond to further consequences. Thus, a compulsive search for relief takes over. With addiction's cycle in place, life without anesthesia becomes vague.

Alcoholism is a slow avenue towards destruction, usually affecting physical, mental, and spiritual health over a span of 30 or 40 years. Heroin is a bit quicker; the life of a heroin addict might last 15 or 20 years. Then cocaine, especially crack-cocaine, destroys at a breakneck speed. Crack-addicts seem to die or go to prison within five years. It really depends on how much money the addict can get their hands on.

Regardless of Jack's defense, his use got worse as he cycled downward in more severe ways. Needless to say he didn't start out using his reported $100,000 per binge in the beginning stage of his addiction. Jack is suffering from a full-blown illness, similar to someone suffering from the depleting effects of cancer, diabetes, or AIDs. In all of these illnesses symptoms continue to interfere more and more with quality of life effecting health, family, emotional status, employment, spirituality, social ties, intellectual functioning, and financial wellness.

Addiction continually escalates causing the emotional and personality changes also to intensify. Eventually the core personality gets entirely buried under addiction's seductive delusions. Denial is always present whispering that current lifestyle is simply the way of the world. All denial is the same, be the addiction vodka, shopping, cocaine, credit cards, or other people. When the explosives of addiction go off on the coffee tables of our lives it is hard to ignore the noise. But from multiple DUI's to Global Warming, addicts are best at ignoring these blasts.

"Addiction is when the action goes from 'want to' to 'have to,' being driven by an urge so strong that one loses control of one's self (one's morals, values, pride) to the point of being willing to do anything to feed the compulsion to the degree that consequences have no meaning nor are they a deterrent; living in a state where the experience is one of a total absence of love and grace, where living in a constant state of fear disguising itself as anger rage, resentment, jealousy, envy, and hatred; a state of existence marked by free floating anxiety and a sense of impending doom. Sounds wonderful, no?"

—Mike, 14 years sober.

4

Finding Common Ground

"When we do not stand up for what we know is right; a part of our being is betrayed.
When we are dependent on anything, we dishonor potentiality.
And, more importantly, dependency undermines self-reliance and self-esteem, the building blocks of peace of mind. When we violate fairness, we violate our hearts.
When we pretend all is fine when it is not, we slam our intellect and our character takes a hit.
Thus, our emotions are then thrown into a downward spiral.
This is where our soul begins to burn and why our spirits die."

—W. L. Houser

James Carroll asks in *Constantine's Sword*, "What kind of ambivalence is it when even the positive aspect is finally revealed as serving a negative end that reveals itself as an absolute?"[15] When the particulars of any mass ideology are dissected, where the intent is to dominate, the thread weaving addiction into place is the common acceptance that is perpetuated regardless of subsequent data proving this commonality to be physically and emotionally debilitating. One of the greatest powers of addiction is the fact that we become like those we are around through a subliminal tendency towards uniformity via the images we are subjected to.

SIM CITY: VIRTUAL OR REAL?

My children play a computer game called 'Sim City.' It is a game that mirrors real life. The goal of the game is to have a nice home, good job and happy family. There are also cheat codes in this game of life to get ahead quick. My children want all the fluff quickly so they use the cheat codes. Jesse my then eight-year-old had a mansion, was married and a working scientist all with in the first hour of the game. In the second hour he lost his wife, his job and his house. My niece Mindy kept having to replace her children because children services would casually stroll on to the screen and walk back off with each new baby. My son Adam lost six of his houses to kitchen fires and all his friends drowned in his pool at a party. They were all baffled at their inability to maintain the quality of life they wanted. Olivia, the youngest, had a great house, happy family and good job. She was the mirror of success at the tender age of seven. Basking in her new found expertise she said Jesse's wife left because he never talked to her and Jesse lost his job because he wasn't trained thoroughly at work, eventually blowing up an experiment in a colleague's hand. He then quit going to work because he was embarrassed, so he lost his house because he couldn't pay the bills. Children Services kept taking Mindys' kids because she stuck them in a room to nap way too much and didn't play with them. Adam kept starting dinner then leaving; thus, he had house fires and he forgot to install a ladder on his pool resulting in the killing off of his neighborhood.

Yet Olivia spent time with her children, talked to her spouse, went to her job, and spent time decorating her house. She created everything our culture teaches us is important; then she was bored and started intentionally throwing pool parties for her neighbors with no ladder in the pool so they would drown and she could create new neighbors. (You have to wonder how many serial killers have this game.) Eventually she graduated to a more analytical game named 'Asheron's Call.' Here she became a warrior but got stuck in the Evil Desert because she lost her sword. So I made the boys help her out as she said demons were chasing her. But after her success at Sim City, the boy's way of helping her was putting her in a dungeon; this is after they severely scolded her for leaving the beaten path and losing her sword. There are a lot of nuances in these games that reveal hordes about our lives.

These games represent the dynamics of culture and teach analytical skills; both are essential attributes in today's world. The kids have to figure out what they are doing and think for themselves: wrong or right, to continue to survive. They occasionally face consequences such as the loss of their friends at the bottom of their pool or being stuck in an evil desert or dungeon. However, they also are rewarded with the trappings of success, which in all reality is what keeps them going on. Many of the things we do in life we do for some kind of payoff. In their virtual lives they simply intended to better themselves, and again, beat each other. (That competition theme runs deep.) Eventually they figure out in order to evolve they must widen their horizons and learn to get along with each other.

THE ILLUSION OF NORMAL

Lifestyle dynamics materialize as many things to many people. For an alcoholic, most of their friends usually drink excessively. For a shopper, naturally, their circle of friends shop as a main activity, an avenue to relaxation, or a cure for boredom. Thrill-seekers hang out with mountaineers. Many suburbanites' drive eight-cylinder SUV's even though the only outback they may navigate is their backyard to wash it. Sailboat enthusiasts stick together and pride themselves on sailing only by the winds of the ocean; powerboat fans because they can speed by the slower sailors in their sailboats. The convergence effect is the point, when it crosses a line that buries individual identity and critical thinking a lethal type of neurosis is fed; a justification of a particular pattern built on the defense of normal, built on the premise that whatever pattern is okay because it is what everyone else does.

Using commonality as an excuse is not an obscure position. And because of this excuse and its particular characteristics many are often the last to know and acquiesce that problematic lifestyle patterns are present. The haze created by normalcy, by a need to fit in, feeds the inability to see belief systems accurately even though many of the specific beliefs are built on a false sense of safety, give a false sense of esteem, and have cracks in their foundation. This blinded stance exists even as one's psyche is next in line for sacrifice. When hiding behind personally monogrammed images of success, antiquated idealism, intellectual pursuits, cynicism or even self-righteous justice, life becomes more and more out of control. No matter how diligent the pursuit for the perfect existence is, it's always riddled with overdrafts, traffic jams, divorces, flat tires, and broken nails.

But perfectionism is a mask addiction wears; a self-imposed, egocentric pressure that is futile because humans are not perfect. In fact, imperfection is woven into the very fabric of creation. In *Lucifer's Legacy* Frank Close states: "The world is an asymmetrical place full of asymmetrical beings. If creation had been perfect and its symmetry had remained unblemished, nothing that we now know would ever have been."[16] At the beginning of the beginning, within our core's core there was imbalance and imperfection. Had matter and anti-matter been perfectly symmetrical we would not exist because matter and anti-matter would have canceled each other out. There would have been only nothingness. But obviously there wasn't; we do indeed exist proving imperfection to have at least one good angle.

LIFE'S MIRROR

Creation, slanted in an asymmetrical way, feeds a reality that proves to be a bit off kilter. When we look into life's mirror the reflection we see is not always what is there. Retailers understand this, which is why they hang mirrors in their stores reflecting slimmer images. Our appearance—looks, clothes, cars, houses, and social skills—are the first impression we solicit and it is by these images we judge and are judged. We tend to desire certain looks, ways, and things as a direct manifestation of avoiding the sting of negative judgment, often accommodating patterns and images that go against our grain rather than deal with the emotional fallout of rejection.

Judgment is another powerful diversionary technique of addiction for the images that we project and use to move through a world bombarded with images, images we consider our armor, can in fact be our Achilles Heel. They can and will turn on us, become our enemy, then own us. How do we know if the props of life have taken over? Our stress and depression levels are good indicators. Built with competitive illusions, images cross a line taking control of our lives moment by moment. Image has become the gauge measuring value even though it is an insanity that teeters on the moods of others. Images persuade us that life is about what you do, versus who you are. The pressure then builds resulting in conflicting foundations, which is the exact recipe for the creation of emotional voids.

When identity is bombarded with images and their corresponding residue, a new species of stress is then formed. Human evolution is altered under such stress. What is deemed normal judgment and desire, the very thing feeding survival, begins to destroy. Judgment is always a two way street. On the terms we judge others, we tend to judge ourselves, only more harshly. Judgment, being the transitory energy that it is, also always changes, what is deemed good one day is bad the next. Yet, even in the midst of judgment's disturbed fallout, we all put our dime in the meter of opinion, this is why judgment is such a powerful weapon of addiction. It is just part of what we do. And, like Tutter's cheese, it is another prime example of how we make our own monsters.

◆   ◆   ◆

Identity is who we are; image is what we present to be. Our core identity is our being, our essence, and the part of us that strives towards deeper meaning. It is the evolution of the mind, spirit, heart, and soul; it is the yearning that empowers us to follow our callings. Identity holds the memory that we are not merely a drop in the ocean, but the ocean itself. Yet, the images of addiction create illusions that proceed in a manner not allowing us to integrate who we are, feeding a sense of separation. Like the cycle of use, it becomes a sinister closed system of perception creating paradigms of thought undermining our lives for a brief surge of pleasure or the illusion of security.

Whether wielding the sword of judgment or feeling its blow, we suffer ramifications. The wall of our psyche is built with judgments and eventually it is these image-fortified bricks that bury who we are and we become off kilter. Eventually judgment is a dead-end endeavor leading us back to spiritual genocide. All the images crack under pressure, materializing as emotional vertigo, which explains why 77% of the adult population is a total mess.

EMOTIONAL JUNGLES

We have established that the cycle of use undermines conscious choice and that the progressive nature of addiction allows it to grow more powerful. Also, we have looked at how images, perfectionism, and judgmental masks bury our core identity suffocating self esteem and spirituality. Now an important point is what happens to the energy of emotions when attempting to pacify them. Most of us have seen the crying drunk or heard statements like "I buy shoes to feel better" or "we took him to the race track to help him forget his divorce." Though these band-aides may alleviate pain in the short term, where does the energy of emotions go when they are shut down? What happens when the addict no longer feels? When self-medication maintains a constant numbing? When rationalization rules? The deeper into addiction one goes, the thicker the emotional jungle becomes.

Emotions are an energy that run through our veins like fire. We can't isolate, expunge or fake them. We must feel them. Emotions are the weakness in our knees or our jump for joy. Built with sensations, emotions reclaim their space in many ways. While under the influence, behavior occurs in a manner that is contradictory to the person that is known—be it an intruder intoxicated with drugs or an out of control consumer guided by the corporate media on a power driven rampage—the anti-social component to an anesthetized life occurs as emotions are sedated.

Yet, emotions continue to manifest. They may reappear simply as clear, constant consequences from poor decisions. Or, they may be subtler, surfacing as uneasiness in the pit of our stomach that wakes us in the middle of the night, an inability to focus, find happiness, or feel contentment in our world. Be it stress that leads to cancer or alcoholism that leads to cirrhosis the manifestation of illness is often directly related to the suppression of emotion.

But emotional consequences can be mediated by expressing the energy of emotions through feelings before the grenade drops. This mediation is often part of any form of an addict's rehabilitation. In most treatment regimes there is a concerted effort to bring emotions to the surface and sort them out. However, these emotions often show up like an eccentric relative, rarely materializing in a manner that is expected, and more times than not, especially for the addict, they take some getting use to.

Emotions are the shadows of our lives, though voiceless; they haunt us as they plow a path through the barrage of data that the intellect piles their way. Yet, they are also a type of moral compass keeping us on course. To medicate them, ignore them, dishonor them, or simply give them a nod and wink then go on without their wise input is to undermine essential guidance allowing the ego full destructive reign and providing an open dialogue for addiction.

MELTDOWNS

Joseph Campbell says in The Power of Myth "I think we are seeking the experience of being alive—the rapture of being alive." Often this sense of aliveness is relayed by the ego. Whether we are at the top of the food chain or residing in low-income housing or if our cubicle has a view or not, egos are the voice that says you can do it, it is the energy behind the force, the crowd cheering, and the rush forging us towards victory. When our egos feel good; we feel good. The god of opinion gives us a gold star, we're deemed a success for the moment and life is good. But, when we lose, when we fall short of some preconceived expectation, our ego turns away from us, quits the game, then takes its ball and goes home. Rejection is never pleasant. This is the fine print on the contract of our humanity. This is when we collapse. This is when addiction's wordy rationalizations cease. This is when something deeper is sought.

As emotional overload ousts the ego we drop to our knees, the moment of despair arrives. Emotions, when not given day to day respect, should we by chance not be blasted by their consequences or not be made ill by their energy have a final trump card to play. After a period of attempting to gain control with intellect, alcohol, power, or purchases they materialize like the skeletons of our lives always do. They eventually become an ominous grand event, having their day in court, instigating a total meltdown.

We are all subject to an occasional meltdown (explaining the high percentage of Americans on medication), but addicts in particular have bigger meltdowns as their emotional stew stays on simmer longer. However, meltdowns are highly underrated. It is this event that tends to say loud and clear "you sir are going the wrong direction" or "ma'am, you should have made a right ten miles back when you took that left." Even though laced with frustration, meltdowns often get us back on track.

And getting back on track isn't always easy. Facing these bottled up emotions includes a degree of bravery, of facing our dragons even if we have to take off our suits, look down manholes, into dark closets or go into the basements of our lives. With the power of our culture's media, it just may mean a total upheaval of not only behavioral patterns but the beliefs upon which they have been built.

◆   ◆   ◆

Identity versus image is similar to reality versus illusion. Yet, often regardless of truth, paradigm thinking rests comfortably in civilizations built on images. Depending on the image, the energy taken to create it or maintain it is all consuming. When the ego is loud and wordy pursuing the dynamics of identity is difficult. When addiction is present, the split waters of the psyche feed image with instant gratification. Dancing on the extremity of reality happens a lot. Looking like a success seems more of a priority than being successful. Identity and purpose are lost to the circling sharks. Addiction is the ego god feeding off of a disturbed form of injustice who eats its own offspring. There is nothing darker that dominates and devours our attention.

"The thing that stands out in my mind about addiction is how insidious it is in regards to its power over my life.
At first it is easily controlled, but then the unpredictability factor causes untold problems in my life. It seems as if this occurs at times when I do have my wits about me as well as in times of stress."
—Joe Lingo, 13 days sober while in Christopher Halfway House

PART II

The Evolution of Dependency

o o o o o o o o o o o o o o o o o o o o o o o o o o o o o o o

"…Against a 'genealogical table which begins in the mud, has a monkey in the middle and an infidel at the tail' most were ready to accept a compromise between The Origin and the Bible.

A Day of Creation might be millions of years long, or might represent six real days that marked the origin of a spiritual Man after the long ages it took all else to evolve. Real bigotry had to wait for modern times.

The creationist movement is part of the triumphal New Ignorance that rules many places, the United States more than most.

In fact, the majority of those determined to tell lies to children believe in Darwin's theory and understand how it works, without noticing.

Evolution is embedded in the American consciousness for a simple and terrible reason.

For the past two decades the nation has lived through an episode that has, with extraordinary speed laid bare the argument of the Origin of Species.

The organism involved was unknown in the nineteenth century but is now familiar.

It is the AIDS virus…

"…The Industrial Revolution was a test of the theory of evolution.

Its results were often expected, sometimes unwelcome and always unplanned."

—*Steve Jones,* **Darwin's Ghost**

5

The Ascent of Control

"The manner of this lust for power has changed through the centuries but its source is still the same volcano…what we once did 'for the sake of God' we now do for the sake of money…this is what at present gives the highest feeling of power."

—Nietzsche

In the virtual world of Fall-Out survival of the fittest does not advance according to normal evolutionary terms. Due to addiction's manipulative powers, a drug called 'Psycho' shifts the game. The glory of Psycho is the fact that it pumps up the losing character, ensuring a win against its once stronger opponent, which is why the availability of this drug occurs when the character is weak and losing a battle. If the character accepts Psycho it makes the character invincible.

Naturally this system repeats itself over and over. The character's sense of invulnerability grows as they defeat all their enemies with great ease, rolling along on a drug-induced, cosmetic high. But eventually a little message comes up on the screen that says, "You are now addicted to Psycho, if you stop using Psycho you will suffer greatly, if you keep using it others will suffer greatly." At this point there is no longer the ability to choose your battles, all interactions are automatically combative until the addiction to Psycho is neutralized, not that this neutralization is an easy task.

Ultimately the issue that surfaces is the fact that the addiction to Psycho includes the user needing more and more to enjoy Psycho's jolt; thus, this need for more gradually becomes part of the character's normal, integrating itself as a mainstay in the character's existence. Like Jack and his clients, their progression includes needing more, finding more, then consuming more. And, as in real life, this need for more also ushers in two distinct ultimatums: Psycho's use will end in either a painful withdrawal from the drug after a sizable amount of destruction has occurred or Psychos use will end with the character's death due to an overdose.

Should the character decide to face withdrawal, the real or perceived weakness that originated the use of Psycho will still need to be dealt with; as with everything else, the original weakness is now more complicated. This side-affect is due to the fact that Psycho's use makes the character stupid as it burns up more and more brain cells with every use; thus, the damage from using Psycho makes it more difficult to confront, articulate, or deal with the original core weakness. This drug-induced delusion of dominance has a high price.

CHANCE

On the Origin of the Species immediately became a bestseller. However, historians tried to keep it under raps because they saw it potentially jeopardizing the power of their secular faith, which shaped culture as it fed industry. Basically this was considered dangerous due to the fact that it had the potential to undermine the progressive control tactics that were gradually being put in place at a cultural level. In spite of the dangers and decisively high stakes it was widely read. A clear description of the evolution of species was now a part of the cultural feed. From primates to primal urges a progressive system built on the energies of life seeking itself and the building blocks of survival were integrated into mainstream thought. Yet, even with the evidence presented in his masterwork, Darwin conceded that there always exists the element of chance in his theory and in evolution itself. This chance, this small bit of leeway in these clear dynamics, is what opens the door to such entities as Psycho and to some of the most powerful issues we face in the 21st Century.

Within our lives we are given many chances and we experience many realities. One reality that is transforming our beliefs and our lives comes in the form of AIDS. Originally AIDS surfaced in the high-risk populations identified as addicts and homosexuals. Some might say, 'Those bad people with bad genes.' Yet AIDS has expanded its clientele and is one of the world's greatest dilemmas. It kills white middle class, rich, poor, Europeans, Indians, and one in every four people in Africa. Western Culture has talked more about protected sex than the early Protestants could have ever feared.

AIDS' devastating power lies in the fact that it continually adapts. It is always changing, confusing researchers, keeping them asking questions versus finding answers. The original virus has so many sub-types that documentation cannot keep up, let alone address the possibility of real treatment or cure. And, even when headway is made, often the virus adapts to its antidote continuing its demise on the body. Natural Selection alters the disease as it progresses, which in turn is what keeps it illusive.

Some say AIDS is God's punishment to man for being bad; to gays for being gay; or to the Africans for being poor, black, or just in the wrong place at the wrong time. AIDS subtly reflects questionable morals of its victims. Regardless of disturbed blame, AIDS' contains in its brief history the entire argument of *The Origin of Species*. As *Darwin's Ghost* states: "AIDS is Darwinism unadorned."

AIDS and moral decline have become the best-known international travelers of the 20th and 21st centuries along with globalization. Globalization's strength, sweeping the world into one huge market, comes as it alters its baseline for normal thus adapting and evolving to maintain its existence—always enticing more consumers, with more products, in more ways. Dependency is nurtured. Addiction, being the multi-talented, ever-expanding precursor to the majority of these well-traveled enigmas, clearly is adding its own color to evolution.

NATURAL SELECTION

Classic evolution can appear to be a ruthless progression, but it does bring forth a cycle where there is normalization, where a balanced status quo eventually surfaces. Even now in Africa some prostitutes are showing tolerance against the AIDS virus that lives in their bodies. They seem to have built immunity to it by subjecting themselves to the virus over and over with multiple partners. Thus, they are the evolutionary dominant species due to their ability to survive this plague. Regardless of the general opinion towards such illicit career fields, unlike addiction, their minds stay intact.

Salamanders show the full circle of evolution as well. Scientists did a study involving salamanders, who normally are mellow creatures eating insects in the ponds along an isolated rim of the Grand Canyon. But when the water dries up, food is then scarce, and living conditions become cramped, these salamanders change. The environmental pressures alter their physical shape and personalities. Muscles enlarge their heads, their mouths become bigger, and they grow a new set of huge teeth so they can eat other salamanders versus the sparse bugs. Basically they become cannibals, but only briefly. Once the population is reduced due to the gobbling up of their weaker neighbors they turn back into peace loving creatures.

Humans often aren't as peaceful as salamanders even in our more placid state. Over the centuries, humans have shown to hold clear potential towards cruel patterns perpetuated by the influence of some type of survival. Darwin told how the people of Tierra del Fuego secured survival and hierarchy. In lean days when food was scarce they would devour their old women rather than their dogs. They needed the dogs to hunt; thus, the wisdom of the elder women fell low on their priority list. Those in power are of an evolution built on brute force and cannibalism. No different than the salamanders, they fed off the weakness of others. Scarcity regardless of form, real or perceived, creates a vicious edge to life where the weaker often become lunch in some form.

PROGRESSIVE GOALS?

A competitive scenario always leaves a winner and a loser. Sometimes the interaction might end with a draw, but this is rare. Within most competitions specific goals, like hurtles to the athlete, are placed along the way. Current capitalistic goals are no different than other competitive goals; there is a long progressive training in place readying the participant for the endeavor. However, we weren't always the fervent capitalists that we now seem to be. The competition many of our ancestors engaged in, though holding the dynamic of survival, was survival against the elements versus survival against one another.

In this now almost obsolete arena most of our ancestors were concerned with producing as many of their daily needs as possible with the use of money being minimal. Credit, which now runs the world, was a rarity. Originally the church closely monitored credit due to the fact that it didn't believe in such things as interest on loans. The church's stance on loans held that loans were for desperate situations, a need not a want, a last resort. Yet, today we get loans for everything. From houses, to cars, to furniture, to food we charge then pay bills; the definition of loan is redefined. The credit card industry in the U.S. illustrates this new stance on loans. Americans have over $1.3 trillion on credit cards tripling the 1992 credit debt.[17] If we want something we buy it if there is room on the credit card. Most people believe in their job security and feel they'll be able to pay their debts. Yet one in six people filed for bankruptcy protection in 1998, up 56% from 1997,[18] and 60% of Americans carry debt.[19]

This debt laden mentality was consistently fed. As belief systems changed, goals took on different characteristics. Rather than self-sufficiency, dependency and decadence took hold. Framed as a way to clarify and predict how the moments of life will go, this dependency took further root in all areas of our lives. Yet this shift entails goals that are geared to please some outside source depended upon to earn a living.

Led by two components, Protestantism and The Industrial Revolution, the shift from independence to dependence gradually became dominant and a new attitude began to form. This attitude was born as a reaction to what was seen as hypocrisy of the church. In Protestantism man could be free from blind-obedience and guided by his own reason with an Inner Light.[20] This was a clear unleashing of earthly ambition. It all seemed good, and it was in some ways, but balance was lost. As Industrialization stepped in, there was a huge push toward getting needs met from outside of one's own self-sufficiency, which grew both physically and emotionally. No longer did we grow our own food; factories and corporations did this for us.

Then as dependency crept into the emotional crevices of life the trade off was clear: we had to earn more money by means of a job to finance the standard of living we hoped for. Money took on a new status; money evolved from a thing to a thought.[21] Money bought satisfaction; it took on God status. A new hierarchy of control emerged as real choice became scarce. And, very importantly, as overt opportunities seemed to increase, life became more slanted in unseen ways.

THE MANIFESTATION OF CONTROL

More and more farms—what once was our freedom—have gone out of business; the control of food has become obvious. In 1850 60% of people who worked did so in some form of farming but today this is reduced to 2.7% of the population. This shift leaves more than 9 million people to live in depressed rural areas across America with no form of income.[22] The government then conspired to eliminate the family farm with various policies. More than 60% of almost $23 billion dollars in federal farm subsidies that is provided to farmers through the Freedom to Farm Act of 1996 went to farm operations that should financially be able to ride out economic fluctuations. According to the

Environmental Working Group, farmers and landowners that make up the top 10% received $14 billion in subsidies from 1996 to 1998, this equals an average of $100,000 each with some receiving more than $1,000,000. The bottom 90% got an average of $6,900. The big guys were paid an average of 27 times more than the little guys.[23]

The little guy surfaces in many arenas and job descriptions and with their back up against the wall of survival he or she must tolerate the intolerable—both in mentality and reality. Walt Disney proves the abuse of workers in both schemes. Disney used this new attitude as an avenue towards mass production. With an appreciation for Henry Ford's assembly line productivity in the automobile industry, Disney ran his factories with a totalitarian style stating, "Hundreds of young people were being trained and fitted," Disney explained, "into a machine for the manufacture of entertainment." Though these factories created cartoons, working at them was less than a pleasant affair. At one point the workers went on strike, hoping to become a union. Disney responded by firing these employees. Disney also staged intimidation, allowing guards to rough up those on the picket line and brought in an organized crime figure from Chicago to impose a phony company union. Disney made a speech to his employees reiterating, "Don't forget this," Disney told them, "it's the law of the universe that the strong shall survive and the weak must fall by the way, and I don't give a damn what idealistic plan is cooked up, nothing can change that."

Following in Disney's footsteps decades later was Ray Kroc who stated his political philosophy as the following, "Look, it is ridiculous to call this an industry," Kroc told a reporter in 1972, dismissing any high-minded analysis of the fast food business. "This is not. This is rat eat rat, dog eat dog. I'll kill'em, and I'm going to kill'em before they kill me. You're talking about the American way of survival of the fittest." Eventually, Kroc donated $250,000 to Nixon's reelection campaign to secure lower wages for McDonald's younger workers. McDonald's workers earned about $1.60 an hour. This new sub-minimum wage proposal reduced some wages to as little as $1.28 an hour.

The Nixon administration also supported the McDonald's bill that permitted McDonald's to raise the price of its Quarter Pounders, despite mandatory wage and price controls restricting other fast food chains.[24]

These events are important as they prove to be a prime example of how legislative actions are shaped by soft monies. Spurring corporate policy making, this chain of events not only proved lethal to individuality, showing the dark mentality at work behind industry, but also initiated everything from corporate greenwash to environmental consumerism to watered-down ecological protection to an army of lobbyist who now sit in Washington shaping policy and legislature towards corporate interests versus the needs of the people, all of this while many of us are waiting in the drive through.

SYNERGY

They bait; we bite. They supply, then we consume; cycling to we demand and they then supply. It is an endless, self-perpetuating system and the essence of consumerism. Anything that is deemed necessary to equate control falls into the category of reasonable. Eric Schlosser sites in *Fast Food Nation* "Among other cultural innovations, Walt Disney pioneered the marketing strategy now known as "synergy." During the 1930's, he signed licensing agreements with dozens of firms, granting them the right to use Mickey Mouse on their products and their ads.... Episodes of *Disneyland* were often thinly disguised infomercials, promoting films, books, toys, an amusement park—and, most of all, Disney himself, the living breathing incarnation of a brand, the man who neatly tied all the other commodities together into one cheerful, friendly, patriotic idea."

Schlosser continues discussing the evolution of Disney's marketing entailing McDonald's climb to domination by again citing Ray Kroc. "A child who loves our TV commercials," Kroc explained, "and brings her grandparents to a McDonalds gives us two more customers."[25] But it doesn't stop here, Schlosser continues to clarify the 'no holds barred' strategy, "Twenty-five years ago only a handful of American companies directed their marketing at children.... Today children are being targeted by phone companies, oil companies, and automobile companies, as well as clothing stores and restaurant chains. The explosion in children's advertising occurred during the 1980's. Many working parents, feeling guilty about spending less time with their kids, started spending more money on them." This marketing grew to a "cradle to grave" strategy hoping to ignite "brand loyalty" in customers as young as the age of two years old. And, it seems to have worked as some market research states that children often recognize a brand logo before they can recognize their own name."[26]

This trend did not progress without the voice of concern. In 1978, the Federal Trade Commission (FTC) tried to ban all television ads directed at children seven years old or younger. Eric Schlosser continues to explain this concern in *Fast Food Nation*, "Many studies found that young children often could not tell the difference between television programming and television advertising. They could not comprehend the real purpose of commercials and trusted that advertising claims were true. Michael Pertschuk, the head of the FTC, argued that children need to be shielded from advertising that preys upon their immaturity." Michael clarifies the crux of the situation with this statement, "They cannot protect themselves," he said, "against adults who exploit their present-mindedness."[27]

Though the FTC proposed a ban, which was supported by the American Academy of Pediatrics, the National Congress of Parents and Teachers, the Consumers Union, and the Child Welfare League among others the ban was not liked by the National Association of Broadcasters, the Toy Manufacturers of America, and the Association of National Advertisers. These industry groups lobbied Congress to prevent restrictions on these children's ads regardless of the impressive voice of concern expressed. Three months after Ronald Reagan was inaugurated, the FTC changed its position on the ban and we experience the full spectrum of its ramifications today. As children we were shaped accordingly and our children are now shaped by this manipulation. A manipulation that is presented as a cultural mainstay and an entry ticket to acceptance in general.

THE PYRAMID

Due to many demands from even more arenas humans have now evolved into a type of commodity. Many of us, dependent, sell our time, our skills, and ourselves to survive. Hooked into a pyramid structure, a system of stagnation where the few on top make money off of those below them, life has become a different type of struggle. Those at the bottom tend to stay at the bottom. In a pyramid system addiction provides security for those at the top. If those towing the bottom stones stay preoccupied they are less likely to do something about the large stones they tow over and over, generation after generation. And very importantly, as we tow stones for money our voice is lost.

The pyramid system is pure control. Though we do not experience the physically suffocating, bone-crushing stones as the Jews once did under Roman rule; our suffocation is more subtle, the picture of our fate presented with a designer frame and a Disney character. Scenes of devastation often feel remote when relayed through the lens of a television camera. Swaying "Kid Kustomers" seems the socially appropriate presentation for what is really going on: brainwashing our children. Though all ages are affected by the onslaught of manipulation, unfortunately, this watered down reality resurfaces with an unexpected, lethal vengeance.

Sara didn't mean to die. Elvis didn't intend to overdose. The kid that shot Johnny didn't consciously plan such an unfortunate fate. Jack didn't plan his constant reentry into treatment. I'm fairly sure that Custer didn't plan a last stand. The Greeks and Sumarians were not intentionally self-destructive. The Roman's loved their empire, though it was in decline due to over consumption, they didn't want to be invaded by German Barbarians. Had they not been so consumed with pleasure, they may have noted the threat the freezing of the Rhine River would create. All facts aside, I'm sure rape, pillage and annihilation wasn't penciled in on the Roman's day planner. None of these people meant to self-destruct. Ultimately they did the best they could, but it wasn't enough for survival.

From individuals to civilizations everyone does the best they can be it with battles, barbarians, great buys, or barbiturates. But in addiction there is an invisible line that exists, and when crossed all bets are off. Then, all of a sudden as we reload our normal, we get nailed. For Custer it was an addiction to glory; his image teetered on an ever-burgeoning ego, which led to more and more lethal excursions. For Elvis it was an addiction to pills to escape pain. For elitist the addiction is power, money and control. Sara just liked to get high but there was blindness to consequences she probably didn't even consider. She probably thought it couldn't happen to her. Jack was always sure the next deal was the one that would make it all come together. They all probably thought the demise each ultimately faced couldn't happen to them due to their limited perception. It seems the inability to look or act beyond the trained response pattern may well be the downfall of 21st century society—Disney character or not.

◆   ◆   ◆

Addiction, when survival based behavior enters into play, manipulates the identity of who is weaker and who is stronger; what were once clear evolutionary dynamics inciting dominance and progression become vague and interchangeable. No different than dealers who create a weaker set of customers by lacing existence with cravings to feed their own perceived needs, the use of Psycho to introduce a scenario where progressive evolution is dismantled, or ads focused at Kid Kustomers, the fittest are quite ruthless. They want what they want regardless of consequence. Darwinism is chemically altered. Survival becomes lost and meaningless to most. Life is now much more complicated. The world of Natural Selection no longer pans out. With many drowning in debt or overcome by futile competition, the fittest are now not only brutal, they are less evolved and generally employed by a logo. As James Carroll says, the cross hairs we stand behind are our own.

"When I first got here I thought you people were so wrong. I thought this place needed help.
It all seemed ridiculous. I thought I was right. The way I lived was right.
And everyone else wrong. I was always so busy making my way right I didn't realize it was wrong."

—Anonymous

6

The Negligence of Excess

"The history of contamination in the environment is simply the saga of a few publicly held corporations on one hand, and government health officials on the other[28]...

When we see nations increasingly doing the corporations bidding, becoming fellow degraders and oppressors, we must ask, 'How is it that our governments protect living, breathing human beings less and less while protecting corporations more and more? By what authority do our governments trade away to corporations the powers and responsibilities of citizens?' We must work strategically to shift government protection from the corporations to the people."[29]

—The Food and Water Journal

Excess is excess no matter how it manifests and regardless of the premise under which it is perpetuated. As John Galbraith states in *The Affluent Society*: "One cannot defend production as satisfying wants if that production creates the want."[30] The archetype of 'I need more' is a self-perpetuating reality that leads back to a sense of want—to something lacking. We are the most physically comfortable people in the world, but also we are the most spiritually uncomfortable.

The Affluent Society continues: "...Beyond doubt, wealth is the relentless enemy of understanding. The poor man has always a precise view of his problem and its remedy: he hasn't enough and he needs more. The rich man can assume or imagine a much greater variety of ills and he will be correspondingly less certain of their remedy. Also until he learns to live with his wealth, he will have a well-observed tendency to put it to the wrong purposes or otherwise make himself foolish. As with individuals so with nations…"[31]

COMPETITION OR SEGREGATION

Desire, when met, creates a 'feel good' sensation. If we win we get what we want, want then feeds desire. Most addicts, when asked why they use drugs, simply respond, "to feel good." Desire can subtly rule who we are; what we do; when we do it; and, how we live. The realization that desire can be a type of personal hell or self-created heaven surfaces with the understanding that it has the ability to block what we need while we are overcome chasing what we think we want. Often comfort levels are conceived in a confusion of circumstance. Then worlds collide; our higher and lower natures meet head on; and bewilderment fills the air.

What happens when desire only feeds desire in a consumeristic culture? What is dominant, higher or lower nature? We know lower instinct is more brutal, as I have said history has shown whole cultures destroyed by such unfortunate functioning. Could such atrocity be repeated under the influence of scarcity thinking? What happens when those who perpetuate the hand of control deem certain life as less deserving? Where exactly are the lines drawn when segregation becomes apparent? What shifts these lines? How are those of us who live outside the walls of the closed communities viewed? When push comes to shove, who will get the resources needed to live in this overpopulated world?

A consumeristic society that is perpetuated for no solid rationale except financial gain and control thrives as enlightenment takes a back seat to getting ahead. Consumerism might be more tolerable if the only consequence was indeed one's own inability to evolve towards enlightenment, but the consequences of excess run much deeper resulting in: disproportionate amounts of waste, social imbalance, environmental degradation, and ultimately the fact that we live on a planet that has finite declining resources and a history of mean-spirited segregation.

The term segregation in itself delineates some type of ambiguous line. The Jews of the Roman Empire fell on the wrong side of the line only because they were not born Romans. The Jewish victims of the Holocaust were born on the wrong side only because they were born Jewish in Europe. The starving peoples of our era fall on the wrong side of a sublime space that dictates who lives and who dies only because of where they happen to live. Though often, in one way or another, their impoverished state is at the hands of corporate, elitist activities. Between 1960 and 1980 28.4 million people were displaced, many left desolate due to their small farms being over run by corporate food production. In India 20 million people were left desolate due to corporate development projects contributing to starvation and malnutrition, which kills 15-20 million people each year. [32] Consumerism under the guise of progress has left in its tracks 25 million environmental refugees as of January 2000. [33]

In a more aware society, there would be no lines, no mass killings due to a vague, undefined segregation, and no excess while others starve. But the idea of enlightenment runs the polar opposite of control. And control is, as it always has been, the ultimate prize. Those in control get the best, live the best, and are the most secure. Those in control can manipulate the highest chance of survival for their personal, politically correct gene pool. Their status as enlightened human beings takes a back seat to an excess-laced negligence.

THE REALITY OF NEGLIGENCE

Within the boundaries of industry's evolution, directly due to the rise of corporate power, there are sixty million people who live within a fifty-mile range of a military-related nuclear waste storage site with many of us unaware that we are located on the wrong side of the line. [34] There also exist reports of three eyed frogs in the Dakotas and of waters swimming with tumor-laden fish. How do these waters affect humans? Is there a connection between buried nuclear waste, landfill contamination, leaking underground fuel storage tanks and deformities or illness?

This question has been answered with an indisputable 'yes.' In 1984 it was found that men living near a Superfund site in Pennsylvania experienced excessive incidence of bladder cancers.[35] A study completed in 1986 has statistically linked children with leukemia in Woburn, Massachusetts to contaminated drinking water due to a nearby waste site.[36] In 1989 the EPA examined 593 waste sites in 339 counties. This examination revealed elevated stomach, bladder, lung and rectum cancers.[37] Another study in 1989, published about Love Canal near Niagara Falls, New York showed how researchers found that children who lived at least 75% of their lives near this notorious toxic dump site had significantly shorter stature and lower birth rate than children not near a site.[38]

In 1990 it was found that increased bladder cancer existed in northwestern Illinois where a landfill had contaminated water supplies.[39] It has been found that there is increased occurrence of leukemia near a toxic dump in North Rhine Westphalia, Germany.[40] At least five studies have shown an increased chance of birth defects for families that live near landfills.[41] On May 28, 1999 Environmental News Network reported: "Miron Quarry, Montreal Quebec has elevated incidence of cancers of the stomach, liver, prostrate, and lung among men, and cervix/uterus among women" again due to environmental, industry incited contamination.

To further clarify a corporate owned, negligent governmental approach to environmental contamination William Sanjour, a former EPA employee, states, "For decades the Westinghouse Corporation disposed of its toxic waste at several dump sites in Bloomington, Indiana. In the early '80s the dumps came under the aegis of the U.S. Environmental Protection Agency Superfund program. While negotiations with Westinghouse over how to clean up the waste dragged on for years, EPA, in order not to upset the negotiations, kept from the public the fact that toxic air levels near the sites were more than fifteen times greater than the Superfund target risk level. At the same time that the EPA was secretly recommending to its staff to wear respiratory protection whenever onsite, it was assuring the people of Bloomington that they were in no immediate danger."[42]

Ultimately, 1400 people die daily from cancer, a disease which virtually didn't exist 100 years ago. Yet we hear about the miracles of cancer research from the pharmaceutical and chemical companies. They identify the daily development of more treatments for cancer. But, what they don't say is that this is mainly because more cancer is surfacing daily. The same companies who are trying to create these treatments often are the ones who perpetuate cancer in the first place with their reckless use of chemicals.

Cancer is a billion-dollar industry; to cure it would put too many people out of work. According to Dr. L. Pauling, two-time Nobel Prize winner: "Everyone should know the war on cancer is largely a fraud." To buy into the idea that corporations and their research really have our best interest at heart seems naive. To thank them for finding reasonable treatments, as in several commercials, seems to border lunacy. Do we thank the guy who rear-ended our car, leaving us in traction, for having insurance to pay the hospital bill?

◆   ◆   ◆

As the Catholic Church turned a predominantly blind eye to the Holocaust, while Jewish men, women, and children were dragged from their homes and taken to concentration camps literally under the Vatican's nose is considered by many as blasphemous. In law, when one knows of a crime that has or will be committed and does nothing it is considered criminal as well. Yet turning a blind-eye happened again concerning the lack of religious positioning against the Vietnam War.

Where does the line of responsibility fall dictating participatory negligence when people are innocently annihilated?

In these times of American excess and waste, isn't it reasonable to align a degree of negligence with the literal contamination or genocide of other people? Isn't it vital to question the manner that we dissect our own traditions and roles? Especially when they have a hand in the harm of others? And, isn't it essential as we question our own excess, if not in the context of how it effects others, at least in how it may ultimately contaminate our lives, our children's lives, and our children's, children's lives? Not only physically, but emotionally and spiritually? Isn't it wise to question who it is that draws the lines to which so many readily bow?

RESPONDING TO EXCESS?

As a response to environmental concerns, Earth Day was established. On Earth Day 2000, 200,000 tons of edible food was discarded; 313 million gallons of fuel was used; 18 million tons of raw material was taken from the earth; 6.8 billion gallons of drinking water was flushed down toilets; one million bushels of litter was thrown out of car windows; 10,000 mink coats were added to the world of fashion; 100 million board feet of wood was sawed up; 250,000 tons of steel was used; and 187,000 tons of paper was used (a lot to print Earth Day Flyers). Also, one out of five people were homeless and hungry as 60,000 children died due to bad water. As Dr. Giuliano states "This on a day of conscious awareness."[43]

The World Watch Institute cautions that seven out of ten biologist believe that the world is now in the midst of the fastest extinction of all living things in the 4.5 billion year history of the planet, as many as half of the species on Earth will die out.Sixteen of the ocean's seventeen major fisheries are collapsing due to supporting 700 million people living in Europe, Japan, and the U.S who enjoy the fruits of industrialization. But the residual of this fruit accumulates. Just one example is a tower of trash on Fresh Kills, Staten Island, which receives 44 million pounds of New York City garbage daily. This mountain of trash continues to grow even with the warning that it would soon become the highest point on the Eastern Seaboard south of Maine and legally require a federal aviation permit as a threat to aircraft.[44] Fresh Kills is only one small example of the legacy we are leaving to our children.

POWER

World Watch Institute, every environmental organization in existence, and many concerned citizens warn of the consequences surrounding Global Warming. Yet, the Bush administration not only is loading its staff with proven enemies of the environment, ignores environmental issues by rejecting the Kyoto Treaty and not limiting CO2 emissions, but also advocates industry's toxic wish list stating more evidence is needed to validate Global Warming's existance; this as he prepares to destroy the last pristine wilderness area by drilling in the Arctic Refuge. Next announced is a position to resurrect the past by increasing nuclear, coal, oil, and gas power plants.

The idea to build 1300 new facilities as a reaction to the current energy problems depicts the strong historical ties this administration maintain with the oil barons and it is not the answer to alleviate the growing consumption of electricity by Americans. This methodology is antiquated, especially in light of the existence and potential use of renewable energy sources and conservation methods. To continue to generate power as we have historically only feeds the problem.

Fossil fuel burning power plants are one of the main culprits of global warming. Electric power plants pump more than 11 million tons of pollutants into the air every year: 1.8 billion tons of carbon dioxide or 35% of the world's emissions (the primary greenhouse gas), 66% of sulfur dioxide emissions (acid rain), 30% of nitrous dioxide (smog), and 21% of mercury and heavy metal contamination which poison freshwater lakes.

The plan to increase this dirty power generation becomes more absurd as it is proven there is enough wind energy in South Dakota, Texas and Kansas to provide the whole country with pollution free energy. And the cost of wind at this time is only between 2.5 to 4 cents per kilowatt-hour. This is not only lower than fossil fuels; it won't rise and fall. Nor does it leave consequences in its trail. At least 40% of the worlds' deaths are because of environmental factors.[45] Every year 64,000 people die prematurely due to air pollution.[46] As a consequence of pollution the hole in the ozone is now 11,000,000 miles wide, which adversely affects the health of over 100 million Americans.[47] If we followed the Clean Air Act a total of $110 billion would be saved in various cost arenas by the year 2010.[48]

In response to these industry-laden plans, there has been an outcry. 86% of Americans state their support for more wind farms. American's do not want more dirty energy sources; yet many are still unaware of ways we can take individual responsibility. Many are unaware of how energy is wasted. Many opt out of putting in solar panels or wind turbines on homes. There are more people with bigger houses in the US than anywhere in the world. Daily thousands of new homes costing between $250,000 and $1,000,000 are built, and built without energy conservation and alternative energy sources. Not only are these homes less than efficient, they are excessive. The average American home is 2500 square feet growing to 4000 square feet, equipped with hot tubs and dishwashers. At the same time 10 million people around the world die each year due to substandard housing, unsafe water, and poor sanitation in densely populated cities.[49] You might say, so what? Where is the connection? How does my comfort affect their discomfort? We affect their discomfort in many ways. A most blatant reason is directly due to severe weather resulting from global warming, which as I have said is dominantly fed by the U.S.

CONTAMINATION

It is in our best interest to take time to become educated on various options. Contamination may fall closer to home than asthma attacks or the premature deaths of 64,000 people. Should personal responsibility happen to fall by the wayside, should we lose focus and not act towards constant support of renewable energy resources, current trends of dirty energy production will dominate. Then what will happen when it is your neighborhood that industries latest brainchild is built? Will a coal-burning power plant be placed in your backyard? What about the noisy diesel burners, which generally are old jet or submarine engines bolted to the ground and are quite loud? Are you prepared to breathe the pollution from the coal burning power plant that is down the street from your house? Experience the acid rain from its SO2 (Sulfur Dioxide) emissions? Drive through the smog that is the result of the nitrous dioxide it pumps into the air?

The lines seem to be clearly drawn: those in far away lands reap the trickle down, but this is deceiving. Why is it that we now have to buy our water? Even with technology many people do not have access to safe water in countries—both developing and industrialized countries. In Vietnam from 1994-1997 only 47.4% of the population had access to safe water, Somalia only 37%, and Nigeria only 49.9%. In the U.S. our access to clean water is slowly decreasing: from 1983-1985 100% of the population had access to good water, then from 1989-1990 only 90% did, then from 1994-1997 it decreased to 73%.[50] We, the elite, have 25% of our population without good water.

Do you know what chemicals your town or city uses to purify the water? Do you know how these chemicals react with one another or foreign chemicals? According to several reports scientists are trying to understand the interaction of chemicals used to make water safe to drink and the foreign chemicals that are entering the water supply from sources such as pesticide and fertilizer runoff.

More questions arise if your water source is derived from a well. What field's runoff might directly contaminate the well? Do you know what aquifer feeds your well or water supply or who else draws from that aquifer? Is there a local corporate farm using excessive amounts with above ground irrigation, then wasting up to 70% due to wind sheers? Is there an ever-expanding gravel pit that fills with water as your well goes dry? Is there a generating power plant using more than its allotment of water to cool its engines, which is draining the aquifer faster than it can be refilled?

Is your well upstream or downstream from the landfill? The nuclear power plant? The resident factory farm? Can any of us turn away from the infiltration of toxins that surround us? Do we ever kick and scream about the waste of this precious commodity? Do you realize that Americans use 1.4 trillion liters a day?[51] Do we consider that when we buy a quarter-pounder with cheese in California it takes about 700 gallons of water to produce that sandwich?[52] Do we educate ourselves concerning the production that is in place to produce that fast food sandwich? Can we internalize the fact that it takes 1,000 tons of water to produce one ton of grain[53] and then takes 16 pounds of grain to make one pound of hamburger? How can we be alerted to the trickle down of consumption?

All of our bad habits are not only poisoning the water but also sucking our water system dry. In the United States farmers are over pumping water from the water tables in many areas. California over used its water at the rate of 1.6bcm a year; this is equal to 15% of the states annual groundwater use. The worse case of over use and depletion has occurred in the Ogallala Water Table which spans eight states in the west and prior to its abuse held water that equaled 200 years of flow from the Colorado River. It is still irrigating a fifth of the farmland in the U.S. through irrigation methods that are wasteful.[54] At current rate of use this aquifer will be dry in 20-40 years. Shifting current irrigation to drip irrigation would reduce water use by 50-70%.[55]

Be it wasting water or wastewater, consequences are hitting us square in the face and they will get worse unless we change our ways. Worldwide nearly 2000 children under the age of five die every year due to diarrhea from drinking polluted water. In developing nations, 95% of untreated sewage is dumped into any water system that is near by. In LA, one treatment plant alone dumps 400 million gallons of partially treated wastewater into the ocean each day causing an unknown number of swimmers to become ill.[56] Our beaches are now lined with "NO SWIMMING" signs.

The average American citizen has 130-180 foreign chemicals in our bodies that our grandfathers did not have. They had one, lead, which naturally occurs in nature. Thom Hartmann clarifies other contributors to our contamination: "According to a recent study, 'most members of the US population contain detectable levels of insecticide chlorpyrifos—a common ingredient in pet flea collars, lawn and garden pest control, indoor foggers, and roach, ant and wasp poisons.'"[57] What are the ramifications of such poisoning? A recent study of four and five-year-old children in Mexico specifically noted a decrease in mental ability and an increase in aggressive behavior among children exposed to pesticides.[58] There has been a 200% rise in children diagnosed with learning disabilities with at least twelve million children diagnosed.

Regardless of data proving the use of chemicals in the environment harmful, pesticide use is up 3000% since WWII. Interestingly enough, crop damage from pests has increased 20%."[59] Even the plant's evolution is swayed by these toxins and not in human favor. Now add to all the former contributions to environmental damage the existence of Agri-business and factory farms who lace water supplies with bacterium.

Sierra Club states, "watching our children drink a glass of tap water or play in a nearby stream should not be a cause for concern. But more families across America are concerned because water polluting corporate chicken, cow, and hog factories are moving in next door. Concentrated animal feeding operations (CAFOs) create one of the nation's most dangerous water pollution problems."[60]

The response? Every hour somewhere in the world a new McDonalds opens up. McDonalds is the biggest consumer of beef and pork, and the second of chicken. Aside from obesity, there is a high price for instant gratification via the fast food route to eating. Thus we must ask; how can 700 million people be protected from the consequences of their own excess? Especially when most are unaware of their own lifestyle trickle down because they are so busy supporting it?

DUE PROCESS?

Often complicating the issue of local contamination is a loss of due process concerning toxins. Peter Montague describes such a case: "As African-American and Hispanic communities have organized themselves to oppose the regulatory-industrial complex, the grass-roots movement for environmental justice has become broader, deeper, more diverse, and much more powerful. It has become difficult for industry and its acolytes in government to find any communities willing to sacrifice their quality of life and the lives of their citizens just so Dow and DuPont can continue making exotic substances for traditional materials (glass, iron, cotton, wool, and wood). The federal government has therefore now opened up a new front in the waste wars. Uncle Sam is working hand-in-glove with dozens of waste companies eager to site dumps and incinerators on lands belonging to native peoples, out in Indian Country."[61]

To further align how individual rights get lost in the marriage of industry and government William Sanjour identifies the EPA's take on 'we the people': "In my 25 years with the EPA, I have heard countless remarks and witnessed many heartless actions denigrating environmental concerns, environmentalists, environmental organizations, and most particularly community environmental activists. While for the outside world the EPA puts on a face of concern and caring for the unfortunate victims of environmental pollution, the agency is permeated with contempt for the same people."[62]

Peter Montague follows on the same premise, "During the past 200 years, corporations have evolved into huge organizations wielding trillions of dollars to achieve their goals. In theory, the marketplace holds corporations in check: If they do something bad they will incur penalties that hurt their profits. However in practice, society has found no effective way of imposing penalties on corporations, so society today has lost control of corporate behavior. Instead of effective control, we have the concept of regulation."[63]

He goes further: "Importantly, corporations have established the principle that chemicals and other new technologies will be considered safe until proven harmful. Thus the burden of proof lies with the public to show that harm is occurring before controls can be considered. (Only in the pharmaceutical industry is the burden of proof reversed. Before new drugs can be marketed, they must be shown to be both safe AND effective. And even with this restriction pharmaceuticals kill an estimated 140,000 (!) Americans each year.)" [64]

But there exists problems when seeking retribution even if harm is proven. In Section 9 of the 'Contract With America' it is required that in any federal court action between citizens of different states, the losing party is obliged to pay the attorney fees of the winning party—even if the losing party is an average citizen and the winning party is Exxon. This section of the Contract also limits punitive damages to three times the economic damages awarded in the case regardless of how gross the misconduct that led to the lawsuit was. The 'loser pays' rule is a bold attempt by corporate America through the "The 'Common Sense legal Reform Act' to jack up the risk of suing it for wrong doing.[65]

♦   ♦   ♦

A researcher observed and compared a picture of a cancer cell and a picture of LA from a certain distance; he noted that they look the same.

Cancer now strikes one out of every three people. Every year 1,200,000 people are diagnosed with cancer.[66] As we become sicker we consume, out of habit, in search of relief, or just because it is what everyone does. Regardless of the degree of consciousness, we are severely affected. And, there are many flash cards, like the LA photo, that are present if our attention would turn that direction. But telling a drunk they need to sober up while they are drunk is futile. The question haunting many, how do you sober up whole nations of intoxicated consumers?

Greg Levoy in *Callings* makes this analogy: "The natives of some Asian countries have a tradition of trapping monkeys by placing a piece of fruit on the ground with a small hole bored in its side, that is tied to the ground. Monkeys reach for the fruit, but by grabbing it, and thereby making a fist, they can't get their hands out of the gourds. The natives then bag them and eat them. If the monkeys would only let go of the fruit they could escape, but for some reason this doesn't enter their monkey minds, and it costs them their lives. We are only a notch up the evolutionary ladder and often act as if we, too, are hardwired with the same suicidal attachments."[67]

"Addiction is a sickness; being stuck; not being able to stop.
It's like using a sharp knife, that you know will cut you, but you
use it anyway with your eyes closed."

—Kenneth, 5 days sober

7

The Evolving Brain

"The man is a marvel, it is a shame about his brains."

—Jewel

Brains are powerful; brain chemistry is amazing. The more I learn, the more I realize that a lot of the patterns we are struggling with as a society and culture can predominantly be explained by the dynamics of brain chemistry. The environmental issues such as air pollution, toxins in food, chemicals in the water, as well as the infiltration of other substances play a huge role in forming our brains, then our behavior, which then affects emotions. Living in what many refer to as a *Prozac Nation,* the altering of emotions has proven to be the bits of those trillion that are non-negotiable.

The way we sense the world around us, then process that information, then proceed to act on that information all involve the brain. If emotion overrides logic, it happens in the brain. If logic and reason prevail, it happens in the brain. If thought is disturbed and overrides reason and feeds chaotic emotion; it happens in the brain. If drugs are used, their influence occurs in the brain.

Addiction screws up the hard wiring of the brain creating a weaker species; this weaker species are then exploited. As Jack sold cocaine all his bets were waged on the existence of a new worldview for the target addict where their choice is restricted; their freedom of thought conditional; and their comfort-levels dependent on drug use. Though Jack didn't understand the particulars of what chemicals in the brain were artificially stimulated, the result is obvious.

CHEMICALLY ALTERED

Depending on the particular drug there are different ways the pleasure center operates. Generally speaking there is introduced an irregular firing of certain brain chemicals such as Dopamine, which sit in the brain stem relaying messages about pleasure. Dopamine via neurons goes from the brain stem to the limbic system at the base of the skull then as far as the cerebral cortex in the front of the head. Thus, the pleasure circuit spans the survival-oriented brain stem; the emotional, primitive limbic system; and the reasoning of the frontal cerebral cortex—quite a wide area providing motivation for everything from basic survival to self-actualization. Dopamine is a major 'feel good' instigator.

Another 'feel good' entity is heroin. When heroin hits the brain it is converted to morphine, which then bind to opiate receptors. These receptors, like dopamine are again within the reward pathways. Morphine has a bit of a double bonus as it also binds to areas involving the pain pathways causing analgesia to occur. Thus not only do we feel good; we don't feel pain. But tolerance occurs in the opiate receptor to morphine. The enzyme that converts the heroin to morphine adapts so that the morphine can no longer cause changes in cell firing—this is the huge glitch to the heroin high.

Cocaine utilizes the dopamine receptors. Cocaine can be free-based to form crack, which increases the addictive quality of cocaine. This is because when Crack is smoked it gets to the brain faster, and the faster a drug affects the brain the more of a tendency it has to be addictive. In Ecstasy the nerve cells that produce serotonin flood the synapse of the brain overwhelming its chemical receptors via the axons creating the feeling of total well-being.

Alcohol's power lies in a profound craving due to its ability to activate and deactivate various areas of the brain. Its secret is its simplicity. It can be made from sugar and water sitting in the sun, which ultimately becomes hydrogen, oxygen, and carbon that together have an unparalleled affinity for the brain. Alcohol dissolves in water and fat, two main components of brain cells. Another secret to alcohol's magic is that it affects five centers of the brain at once. All at the same time it will reduce anxiety, create euphoria, induce a level of sedation, decrease inhibitions, decrease coordination, and affect aggressiveness, forgetfulness, and memory.[68] Because alcohol is legal we rationalize its use as normal. Alcohol is a multi-trillion dollar industry that buys a lot of influence towards a perceived normal. Legal or illegal, with the repeated use of mood altering patterns dependence occurs.

Whatever gets your endorphins, dopamine, and serotonin cooking, at some point a line can be crossed that makes the pattern no longer a *choice* towards pleasure but a *compulsive behavior* towards pleasure. Ultimately addictive based reactions, initial behaviors, and navigational abilities are the concrete workings of instinct. Instinct always gravitates towards survival in the least painful, most pleasurable manner. The mind doesn't generally have a say until the details of instinct are trained, which is difficult while in the arena of the pressure cooker type of dynamics that an existing chemical imbalance creates. Basically, if backed up against the wall of survival, an addict will do whatever it takes to stay alive in the easiest manner available.

TRIGGERS

A trigger is something that ignites a feeling in such a way that the sensory experience and the emotions therein override intelligence. A consistent use of any drug or a continual employment of any pattern is the most powerful trigger in the world because humans are creatures of habit. For Ray and my friends it is power and money. For Jack it is crack-cocaine the scenic route, for some people triggers are visual images in the mind. For others it is a street or money or people associated with a certain feeling. Triggers are physical and/or emotional longing for induced relief from stress or sadness or depression or just feelings in general. All triggers bring back the essence of a pleasurable experience while erasing all the bad things that occurred in the experience's aftermath. All mood-altering endeavors—be it drugs, alcohol, shopping, money, or power—have a set of triggers.

Triggers are the foot soldiers of addiction. Triggers can eliminate existing decisions. In the subconscious paradigm, triggers dominate in a manner that takes the addict from trigger to the use of some drug in one sweet step. A trigger can also be a chemical imbalance. The very nature of drug use depletes various chemicals in the brain such as dopamine and serotonin to a degree that create deficits. It takes time for these deficits to stabilize. Thus, some degree of withdrawal and depression is experienced directly due to an addict's use. Similar to mental illness, brain chemistry is altered in a manner that creates less than par functioning. Triggers take over behavior. Knowing someone's triggers is power.

TOLERANCE

One of the most powerful triggers in existence is simple tolerance. The definition of tolerance is the need for more of something to attain the same emotional or physical results as attained by a smaller amount used previously. Tolerance is a physical adaptation due to the use of something over and over again. In the case of tolerance, the trigger is an attempt to gain relief from the pain of withdrawal. Needing relief from pain happens because the neurons adapt to the repeated drug exposure and only function normally in the presence of the drug. The character in Fall Out built up tolerance to Psycho. Jack counts on the ramifications of tolerance to cocaine to increase his profit. Due to tolerance individual consumer demand is also always on a steady rise.

Tolerance is derived from the fact that if you drink a six pack of beer a day for a month, the next month it will take seven beers a day to obtain relaxation or relief. Then the next month it will take eight beers to accommodate the goal of relief. Tolerance creates the need for more of whatever to maintain status quo. As tolerance grows to whatever drug, taking more and more to satisfy addiction's appetite while the very indulgence that seems to bring relief in all actuality is the cycle that is the building blocks of addiction's genius. Tolerance breeds craving and craving breeds tolerance, this is as tidy and progressive as nuclear waste.

Craving is an amazing, discombobulating animal that creates an experience of confusion and overrides all intellectual sense. Craving resides in instinct occurring with everything from chocolate to alcohol to a new suit or dress or power or a lover or toys or houses or for those like Hannibal, others for murder than a meal. I remember hearing one serial killer's comment on his obvious inability to not kill: "It is compulsion, from urge forward I was out of control." Craving and compulsion walk hand in hand. Be it consumers or addicts or serial killers the rationalizing and manipulations of cravings shift perception to a frequency which pursues the fix.

When tolerance and cravings are present, life is crazy. Overwhelmed, relief is sought again and again at the command of craving in various degrees. Cravings are the brain's way of responding to conditioning. It is the brain's way of saying things here aren't like I'm use to. Depending on conditioning some cravings are subtle and manageable while other cravings make rational beings into monsters. Cravings create stress. There is a method to the madness of a monster created by stress because of the brain's response to stress. The chemical ramifications in the brain of stress are extremely powerful and very scary in light of today's culture.

THE CHEMISTRY OF STRESS

We all experience stress and we all experience environmental pollutants. But how do these pollutants affect brain activity? How does it play out in our brains and eventually in society as a whole? Mental pollution is the culmination of unnatural stimulation of the brain via stress and the infiltration of foreign chemicals, which are often toxic pollutants. It is not news that if someone drinks contaminated water, breathes polluted air, or eats food that has not been proven safe there is going to be fallout. The fallout of certain environmental degradation literally settles on the brain, which then induces a whole new scenario.

The brain responds to stress with the hormone adrenaline, similar to the way the brain responds to bad experiences. When adrenaline shows up in the brain it makes the body ready for action: that fight or flight scenario. Yet, when this hormone is overactive as a result of persistent stress it becomes a sort of terrorist taking over genetic regulation. The terrorized gene than sets up deviating networks between brain cells, imprinting how the brain has miss-learned, imprinting the craving for relief, and imprinting faulty instinctually based reactions. This misnomer of reactions is huge as these responses manifest in such ways as: epileptic seizure verses clear signal between cells, an episode of depression versus happy thoughts, or a surge of rage rather than an ability to compromise.[69]

Another stress related ramification to our brains involves serotonin. Scientists have discovered that stress brings to life a mutant serotonin gene that then induces the disorder of depression due to a faulty, reduced level of serotonin being released in the brain. If there is low serotonin and low noradrenaline there is high risk for suicide. Thus, medication is needed to stabilize mood and relieve depression.[70] Depression rates have risen steadily since the 1940's. We kill ourselves off more than any other country in the world. Another offshoot of the altering of brain chemistry via stress identifies that with low serotonin and high noradrenaline a high risk for aggression if not violent behavior towards others exists. According to the FBI between 1960 and 1991 the U.S population increased 40% and crime increased 560%. Murders increased 170%, rapes 520% and aggravated assaults 600%.[71] The marriage between stress and environmental pollutants is an explosive one.

THE PSYCHOLOGY OF POLLUTANTS: CREATING THE VIOLENT MIND

Does pollution cause people to commit violent crimes? Can environmental pollutants that settle in the brain also explain the increase in such crimes as homicide, aggravated assault, sexual assault, and robbery? Lead causes poor impulse control and learning disabilities. A history of learning disabilities cause stress and we know stress affects the brain negatively.

To prove the point of these toxic pollutants Roger D. Masters developed the neurotoxicity hypothesis of violent crime. According to his hypothesis, toxic pollutants such as the metals lead and manganese not only cause learning disabilities and an increase in aggressive behavior, but cause loss of control over impulsive behavior. These traits combined with poverty, stress, alcohol and drug use, as well as social factors produce individuals who commit violent crimes.

Ultimately, what Master's has proven is that individuals who engage in criminal behavior are more likely to have absorbed toxic chemicals than a comparable control population. He did this by citing studies showing that low-level poisoning by lead and manganese are associated with learning disabilities and attention deficit disorder. He reiterates that these are in themselves associated with deviant behavior. He cites seven other studies showing that violent prisoners have significantly elevated levels of lead, manganese, cadmium, mercury or other toxic metals, compared to prisoners who are not violent.[72] With this data there is the ability to predict future violence in people exposed to toxins.

Masters continued to prove his findings utilizing data from FBI files on violent crimes in all the counties of the U.S. He correlated this with data on industrial releases of lead and manganese into the environment of each county, using data from the U.S. Environmental Protection Agency's TRI (toxic release inventory) database. Masters split all U.S. counties into six groups—those with and without industrial lead releases; those with and without industrial manganese releases; and those with higher-than-average or lower-than-average rates of alcohol-related deaths. After controlling for all the conventional measures of social deterioration (poverty, school dropouts, etc.), Masters found that counties having all three measures of neurotoxicity—lead, manganese, and high alcohol—have rates of violent crime three times the national average. In other words, environmental pollution and alcohol use have a strong effect on violent crimes, completely independent of any of the 'traditional' predictors of violent crime, i.e. poverty, poor education, etc.

The presence of pollution is big a factor coloring the lives of those raised in poverty stricken areas. Aside from influencing criminal behavior, there is a type of trigger or commonality that exists. This common ground can be found in the breaking down of the inhibition mechanism. In a polluted brain all impulse control disintegrates. Thus, where there is no impulse control, again, instinct rules. When instinct has been altered via brain chemistry to respond to certain triggers—be it a stress altered brain or drug cravings there lies the key to violent behavior.[73] Thus, the largest issue of all, as Masters believes and has shown, is that when our bodies and brain chemistry is altered by exposure to toxins we lose a natural restraint that normally holds our violent tendencies in check. At a cultural level, looking at the degree of stress and pollutants in our country, these are astronomical findings.

Research studies show why we can't ignore the way evolution occurs: from mutated serotonin genes to peace-loving salamanders growing fangs and eating their neighbors to cocaine addicts. Salamanders' turning vicious just doesn't seem progressive. Mutant genes seem a little bit over the top. A chemically altered environment causes problems. Meat-eating salamanders would eventually cause problems for others as well as the weaker salamanders. Too much pleasure and we probably wouldn't be here because we would have been too preoccupied with pleasure to survive the evolutionary treadmill. Yet not enough pleasure leads to stress and lack of will to survive. The make-up of the brain is indeed evolving. But is it evolving for the better?

◆   ◆   ◆

Former U.S. Surgeon General C. Everett Koop has said, "Regarding violence in our society as purely a sociologic matter, or one of law enforcement, has led to an unmitigated failure. It is time to test further whether violence can be amenable to medical/public health interventions."[74] Across the board toxicity is being seen as a block in evolutionary terms for many. Until we clean up our act, we will see violence and drug use increase in our society.

It is consciousness that separates humans from other animals. When humans can no longer consciously choose to behave in a specific manner, when they no longer engage the frontal cortex's reasoning, all behavior is driven by instinct, by a lack of impulse control, and most importantly by the pleasure center of the brain: either seeking pleasure or seeking to avoid pain. Addiction holds close company with an animalistic form of survival whose merciless control ultimately defines who lives and who dies.

"I once knew a girl who fell deeply in love at the vulnerable age of 15; her partner was drugs.
The girl would look at you with wide dark eyes that seemed to plead for understanding while pushing you away. There wasn't room for much else in her life...."

—Patti Davis, Dope: A Love Story, Time May 7, 2001

PART III

The Power of Influence

o o o o o o o o o o o o o o o o o o o o o o o o o o o o o o o o o

"The media—TV, radio, newspapers, magazines, even bill-boards—are deeply involved in your personal life for much of your waking hours. The media keep you company, and they can entertain, inform and inspire you. That's good. They can also shape your opinions, behavior, tastes, and desires. That's not so good. And they can be used by powerful people to seduce and persuade you and often lie to you. That's dishonest, sometimes downright evil and always there in your face."[75]

—*The O'Reilly Factor*
Bill O'Reilly

8

Perception Screens

"Unnatural deeds do breed unnatural troubles."
—William Shakespeare, 'Macbeth', Act V, Scene 1

In the early 1990's a seventeen-year-old kid was sentenced to life in prison for killing a sixteen-year old for the $125 pair of Nike Air Jordans he had on. The killer had seen these shoes on TV and wanted them. So this kid-killer put a .22 caliber pistol to the head of one Johnny Bates, pulled the trigger, and walked away in a new pair of high top, designer brand tennis shoes. When did the belief that killing is bad get lost in this kids head? Or, was it ever taught at all? I think we can make an educated guess that he was taught that killing was in the not-okay realm of behaviors; yet, he killed. And, he killed for a pair of shoes that he didn't need, but simply wanted.

At the trial the defendant's attorney stated: "It's bad when we create an image of luxury about athletic gear that forces people to kill over it."[76] I don't buy for a second that anyone forced the shooter to pull the trigger; but I do contend that the effects of advertising had a role in a belief system that led to such behavior. I do contend that this gun carrying kid was influenced. His mind was affected in the same way the character using Psycho was affected. Like Jack the drug dealer, Nike's advertising to some degree intentionally ignited a craving for their product. A craving that turned lethal.

COLORING PERCEPTION

Human beings do the best they can with the information they have gained from their lifestyle, culture, family, traditions, education, environment, and genetics. We sense the world through a screen or map that is composed of stored experiences, memories, and thoughts. This screen is our internal map to the world giving us the strategies we need to get from A to B to C—be the strategy a rationalization for a particular behavior, a response to certain stimuli, or a navigational plan to get through the day—this screen's coloring of our emotions, beliefs, abilities, and responses ultimately create how we move through our days and nights. The building blocks of these screens materialize in many ways, some more harmful than others.

Jack's map was a rich array of choices that narrowed with each crack-cocaine binge. Ray became an anti-social element of society due to his ego's dependence on an identity derived from bogus, illegally financed programming. The shooter in the Johnny Bates story may have been subjected to massive amounts of media, advertising, and violence; thus, creating a perception that rationalized an act of violence for a pair of shoes as reasonable. My friends, as with many in a monetary society, are greatly influenced in the belief that there is not enough, medicating it by always pursuing more. The determination of how much our perception screen is colored depends on whom or what is doing the coloring.

The manipulative ability of the media is no secret. Media's influence is literally done by, as Walter Lippmann says, placing "pictures in our heads." From TV to bumper stickers to ads to billboards or where ever our eyes linger, we are overwhelmed with images that can boycott any sense of identity. The attack begins at a very young age, before we can even identify that the enemy has crossed into the sacred ground of our subconscious mind. Before we know what surrender is, a part of our soul has surrendered. Then it surrenders some more. We then realize, briefly, that we just may be in the midst of a mesmerizing fog. But cultural cravings are now in the driver's seat and we quickly change channels.

MESMERIZED

U.S. government sells the American way abroad by hiring more than 8000 people to create propaganda that makes the U.S. look good. They do this with 90 films, 12 magazines in 22 languages, and 800 Voice of America programming in thirty-seven languages with an estimated audience of 75 million who all hear the virtues of the American way.[77]

U.S. food's advertising budget averages around $30 billion a year. Marketing is a method to convey the usefulness of products. Advertising fills the gap from common sense to sedation and we buy what we must run off, starve off, sweat off, or have sucked out eventually. Americans spend $33 billion on diet products to take off all we eat[78] and average $400 million worth of liposuctions a year.[79] Dr. Graham Colditz of the Harvard Medical School summarizes the direct and indirect cost of our obesity to be $118 billion.

Kellogg spends $40 million on advertising. Though expensive, they add to our perception screen's color, especially in children. Today over 5000 schools have contracts with the fast food industry to provide food in some form[80] creating more cravings in children at a young age. Schools are signing contracts with Taco Bell, McDonalds, Coke, Pepsi, and many others for extra money to fund school activities. Also shaping a very young perception screen in a specific manner. Realistically speaking this is over $30 billion to sell us something we need in some fashion, but not necessarily in the fashion that is healthy.

Of all media, the TV is most powerful in altering perception. It implants thoughts and cravings on a mass scale. Most Americans watch 30 hours of TV a week; this is about 37,822 commercials per year, which works out to more than 100 TV ads a day.[81] The TV sends out flashes of light to which the brain, also being electric, responds at many levels. Hypnosis is accomplished with the use of flashing lights. Thus, this is not an ambiguous idea but a real electrical force. Nuero-physiologists trace the pathways of images into the brain, then into cells.[82] We are physically altered by these images. This is why a movie sticks in our heads. This is why a scene overwhelms us. This is how we recall its details infinitely. The power of these images in our brains is why we scream, cry, jump, change our hair, clothes, or diet until we are ill; it is also why many yell at their kids to be quiet so they can watch TV.

If still questioning the power of TV, consider the fact that most people will view about 2,000,000 commercials by age 65. In retrospect, we could probably look back and see the choices influenced, created, and changed by advertising. The power of advertising should not be minimized in any arena. With all the media put together one is likely to hear or see 100-300 ads a day and receive an average of 216 pieces of direct mail and advertising. This does not include the countless billboards, bumper stickers, and displays. This influence is the ammunition utilized to not only control, but steer many in a specific, consumer-laced existence.

REALITY OR FANTASY

At a cellular level TV has become a sort of lifeline to our emotions. As pretend images and real images are both stored in the same cells of the brain, their influence can initiate a type of disorientated perception creating new baselines for acceptable or non-acceptable behavior and increasing what it takes to shock us. Even with the obvious increase in violence, the media responds with more violent images, accommodating this shock tolerance. The Johnny Bates story reflects this clearly. In this story the details—the very details that are supposed to differentiate between fantasy and reality—got more confused, priorities and baselines grew vague, the brain then accommodated, and some real problems were created.

The brain, struggling to establish the difference between all the details of movies from all the details of memory and reality, experiences a disorientation as well as stress. As these various images become confused, the ramifications are complicated and multifaceted. The influence of images especially during the years of development, become an intricate part in the brain's formation. This dynamic is why so much concern was voiced against TV. Yet due to communal acclimation these are the exact years that many of our children sit in front of the TV to be baby-sat. The brainwashing that exists in these early years not only feeds the brain in a manner that sets it up for a predisposed vulnerability towards subconscious influence and light generated imagery, it detracts from the brain's ability to build more analytical, empathetic pathways. Kid Kustomer might be a catchy synonym, thrown around as a clever marketing tool, but its ramifications again prove to hold unseen consequences.

Thom Hartmann clarifies, "converting words to pictures is most powerfully learned by hearing stories (rather than watching cartoons, Nintendo games, etc.). Children who do not hear stories when they're young experience a developmental stunting, and permanently lose their ability to visualize, imagine, and to a large extent, empathize. {Empathy is the cornerstone to compassion.}"[83]

Explaining the consequence of a lack of empathy he continues: "It is true that seeing over a dozen violent images an hour on TV can cause children to grow up tolerant (and maybe enthusiastic) about violence. A profoundly destructive consequence of using TV as a baby-sitter has now produced a generation of children lacking in critical thinking skills (so they readily march to the tune of corporate or political agendas that are presented in one sentence slogans) and lack imagination (so they don't question the "wisdom of being a good little corporate drone in a corporate world)."

THE SELL

If you question the power of influence, one of the biggest symbols of the power of relayed imagery directly due to TV is the continually rising sales of SUVs. I recently had a friend buy an SUV. I asked him why he bought it in these times of concern about global warming, especially with the fact that he knew its CO2 emissions were three times greater than smaller, more economical vehicle. He explained, "My new vehicle can get through snow like anyone's business, and the fact that it is bigger than most other vehicles I have a better survival rate in case of an accident."

I mentioned in return "You live in the Southeast, you get very little snow."

"Better safe than sorry." He rebutted.

"What about the accident rate due to faulty tires?"

He replied, "They have gotten that under control."

"Aren't you concerned about Global Warming?"

He said, "Of course I am concerned, but how much affect will this one vehicle have? At some point you have to draw a line from which decisions are based on one's needs versus the needs of all. This is one of those times. I needed a dependable vehicle. I deserve to drive what I want." Then he gets to the root of the attraction: "Besides, I feel good when I drive it. I feel powerful. And, if any of that road-rage comes my way I'll smash'em like a bug. In my new vehicle I am protected, I am the biggest and the baddest on the road. In these days of violence, this gives me great comfort.

There was an article in the New York Times on August 6, 2000 introducing the 'Hummer' a steroid doused SUV. The sale tactic went something like this: 'The Hummer is a vehicle for the rugged INDI-VIDUALIST who wants to IMPRESS HIS/HER friends with stories of going into rough terrain.' People bought into this pitch with the image of 'Individualist' while ignoring the fact that these Hummers are huge in creating more air pollution and use excessive amounts of fuel.

When it comes to wasting energy, SUVs are unrivaled. Built with outdated, gas guzzling technology, most SUVs get just 13 miles per gallon. Thanks to this dynamic, automobile CO2 emissions exceed pre-1980 levels. The Hummer ad is a prime example of how the auto-industry advertising portrays SUVs as the ticket to freedom and the great outdoors feeding a disturbed type of image IV. Commercials depict the SUV driver as going through the Arctic, climbing mountains, or tearing through desert sand dunes. The owners are suddenly brave warriors. Or, as my friend seems to feel, they are protected due to an oversized vehicle.

The Sierra Club article continues to clarify the nature of the SUV: "In reality, the only off-road action many of these vehicles see is accidentally driving through a flower bed next to the driveway. Missing from these ads are other contributions from SUVs—the brown haze of air pollution hanging over many of our national parks, images of weather disasters linked to global warming or the oil derricks and tankers needed to feed gas-guzzling SUVs. In contrast to Detroit's carefully crafted image, SUVs have a dark side. They spew out 43 percent more global-warming pollution and 47 percent more air pollution than an average car. SUVs are four times more likely than cars to roll over in an accident and three times more likely to kill the occupants in a rollover. They also cost the owner thousands more on gasoline."

CULTURAL CONVERSATION

The SUV represents a component of current day, illogical trend setting. It supposedly represents a successful image in today's society. At different times throughout history there are various cities that represent American spirit, with changing images driving these eras. In the late 1700s Boston proves to be a place of political radicalism. Spearheaded due to a shot that was heard around the world. (Are you pulling up the visual of the minuteman and his musket?) Then in the mid-1800's it is New York with its melting pot theme that became symbolic of America. Naturally the Statue of Liberty is the emblem in this case. Then in the early 1900's, Chicago proves dominant (notice we are gradually moving west) as the city with big shoulders and heavy winds; it came to symbolize the industrial revolution and a dynamic America.[84]

In the twentieth century for all productive purposes Las Vegas is the poster child city. With its huge casinos, massive gambling, nightclubs, and even a pyramid it shows how our culture shifted public discourse—politics, religion, news, athletics, education and commerce—to that of entertainment, pleasure,[85] and subliminal seduction. It represents our abundance and ability to squander it reflecting a gravitation towards a type of pleasure that includes gambling with our lives. With these traits in place we make our way from ocean to ocean in the two centuries of our country's history. Here we find that Los Angeles and Hollywood represent us. Actresses, actors and athletes mesmerize us; they are our stars. We try to dress like them, cut our hair like them, and we live vicariously through the plots of their shows.

Culture is like a huge conversation. Cultures send and receive messages within themselves and to other cultures just like people do. Plato made important observations about conversation 2300 years ago. He postulates that how we are obliged to conduct a conversation will have the strongest influence on what ideas we can conveniently express. And the ideas that are easy to express will become important in that culture.[86] Our ancestors looked at the stars, sky, moon, and sun and hoped for freedom. We have freedom and choose to look at TV. We can choose any vehicle, yet many pick polluting SUV's.

◆   ◆   ◆

As a direct result of advertising, which has nothing to do with 'need' and everything to do with the media created and manipulated 'want' poor decisions are often made concerning purchases. These purchases are not only expensive, but a type of inflationary-based prison. What is seen as truth or reality on TV affects the mind, altering knowledge, maps, beliefs, truths, and ultimately lifestyles. Commercialism is more than a snappy tune or Disney character. It is a subliminal type of persuasion, a real threat for democracy, deadly for Johnny Bates, and a form of violence. Yet it is mainstream America and accepted as normal.

"I knew the first time I put a needle into my arm that I was an addict. It was my escape.
It was how I avoided looking at reality. I felt a lot of self-hate.
Then there was always a crisis that lead to reaching out to others.
Yet I always seemed back at it.
Time after time, more bad things happened. Finally I stayed straight."

—Phyllis 3 years clean and sober.

9

Persuasion and Presentation

*"If serious reading dwindles to nothingness, it will probably mean
that the thing we're talking about when we use the word 'identity'
has reached an end.'*

—Don DeLillo

Around 323 BC Aristotle reconciled the view of the Sophists and
the position of his teacher (Plato) in *Rhetoric,* the first comprehensive
theory of persuasion. For Aristotle, the purpose of persuasion was to
communicate a point of view. Aristotle believed that knowledge could
only be gained by the use of logic and reason and that not everyone was
able to reason clearly about every issue. So Aristotle felt the truth
needed to be communicated in a certain manner to the 'denser souls'
so they would come to the 'right' conclusion. The Romans picked up
the tradition of 'decision by persuasion' and took it one step further by
employing professional persuaders.[87] Today we have come to know
these persuaders as lawyers and politicians.

The Puritans had to contend with their own dose of weekly persuasion. They sat through an average of 300 sermons in their lifetime,
most lasting more than two hours. Some churches had an enforcer
walking around ready to nail any parishioner who might fall asleep. At
about the same time, early American patriots spend the summer of
1787 debating what would become of the U.S. Constitution, then produced for the newspapers eighty-five articles totaling some 600 pages in
its defense. Today a political advertisement, be it informative or a
slam-dunk on the competition, runs thirty to sixty seconds (about the

time it takes for a quick drug deal). Not only has presentation changed, so has content.

TAINTED TRUTH

Persuasion can be overt or covert. The way research occurs and is presented is a type of covert persuasion different than subliminal feeds. This type of persuasion surfaces in the dynamics of how information is gathered and disseminated. Cynthia Crossen writes in *Tainted Truth*: "Behind the explosion of corrupted information is, first, money."[88] For several decades after World War II information was largely gathered and submitted by scientists who were funded by government or academic institutions. Unfortunately, there has been a shift. There is less money out there for governmental sponsored research and more scientists wanting to complete research. In this imbalance corporations and companies arise employing their own researchers. Though there is an outward statement of unbiased gathering, reviewing, and disseminating the data, there is also the reality of who the researcher works for and the spoken or unspoken expectations.

Independent research is becoming a rarity in today's high tech, big business world. We are taught to trust doctors, yet regardless of overwhelming evidence there are still doctors who deny the connection between cancer and chemicals. So who are these doctors? Who employs them? They are employed by chemical companies or financed by them. Credibility of the researcher is not in question here, ethical behavior is. (Though naturally credibility is harmed when aligned with unethical behavior. Back to the suspicious war on cancer.) The credibility of research findings, when the research project is financed by a certain entity brings to question the ethics of the project.[89]

Another questionable component of research is how questions are asked, and in what order they are asked. The way questions are ordered can create what researchers call a 'response effect.' These effects come from the fact that when you query humans all kinds of things influence the response, everything from incorrect memory recall to emotions. And the ultimate factor: as humans we tend to answer in a manner that is more on the egocentric edge than in a balanced, centered way.

Gallup Polls play by these same rules. For instance a poll has stated that 62% of Americans feel we shouldn't get rid of the penny; the little known detail was that the poll was sponsored by the zinc industry. Another Gallup poll stated that a business is more successful if a cell-phone is used—data sponsored by Motorola.[90] In *Tainted Truth* she goes on to say that there are categories of words identified as 'purr-words' or 'snarl-words.' Then she uses this example: "A young monk was once rebuffed by his superior when he asked if he could smoke while he prayed. 'Ask a different question, a friend advised, ask if you can pray while you smoke.'[91] The various ways we phrase our words are powerful; as is the way we receive and process interactions.

Finally, the language used is a determining factor in research results. Cynthia Crossen uses the examples of: "MX missile or Peace-keeper, Pro-choice or Pro-abortion, Welfare or Public Assistance, Department of War or Department of Defense or Environmental Racism or Environmental Justice."

ENVIRONMENTAL JUSTICE

The term 'Environmental Justice' evolved a decade ago due to many people living in areas that were dangerous to their health. This danger exists because of the chemical poisoning of the environment from industries that were also located in these places. The pollution tends to be located mainly in the areas where poor people, mostly of color, live. As industries took up residence they justified locating in these poor communities stating they would provide "potential" benefits from increased job availability. Yet, the real underlying motive proves that industry executives also believed that these communities, because of their low class and economic status, would not protest the harm that might come from environmental pollution and mishandling of wastes.

A prime example of this corporate attitude and behavior can now be found in what is called 'Cancer Alley,' a section of the Mississippi River between Baton Rouge and New Orleans.

In the early 1990s the U.S. Environmental Protection Agency (EPA) became involved with this issue of corporations poisoning poor communities. The movement proclaims they should have access to the same type of environmental quality as middle and upper class communities. When this topic first came on the national scene, it was referred to as 'environmental racism.' After the EPA's involvement in this dilemma, while trying to find solutions to these very complex problems, they felt it political suicide to be involved with a 'racist' issue, and therefore renamed the movement 'environmental equity.' But what did equity mean to the poor people living in the communities where this was going on, where their families were slowly being poisoned? In response, the EPA decided to rename the movement again, this time calling it 'environmental justice.' After all, even the poorest, most illiterate people could understand what justice meant.[92]

GREENWASH

Another response to obvious offenses of corporatism is 'greenwash.' Greenwash is a bunch of corporate lies posed as truth to control image damage for the destruction big business creates in the world. Jed Greer and Kenny Bruno state in *Greenwash the Reality behind Corporate Environmentalism,* "A corporate leader in ozone destruction takes credit for being a leader in ozone protection. A giant oil transnational embraces the "precautionary approach" to global warming. A major agrochemical manufacturer trades in a pesticide so hazardous it has been banned in many countries, while implying that it is helping to feed the hungry. A petrochemical firm uses the waste from one polluting process as raw material for another, and boasts that this is an important recycling initiative. A logging company cuts timber from natural rainforest, replaces it with plantations of a single exotic species, and calls the project "sustainable forest development." And these corporations, with the help of their business associations and public relations firms, help set the agenda for global negotiations on the crises of environment and development."[93]

These companies include DuPont who waited 14 years after scientists first linked CFCs to ozone destruction before it agreed to stop making them. Royal Dutch/Shell Group, who explores oil, owns 400 million acres in 50 countries, employs 133,000, and has annual sales of around US $100 billion with US $9billion in cash reserves yet leaves devastation in the trail of its definition of progress. As Ken Saro-Wiwa states in the November/December 1995 issue of *The Ecologist*: "At the root of my travails lies Shell, which has exploited, traduced, and driven the Ogoni to extinction in the last three decades. The company has...left a completely devastated environment and a trail of human misery. When I organized the Ogoni people to protest peacefully against Shells ecological war, the company invited Nigerian military to intervene...I have one suggestion for those whose conscience has been disturbed by my story: boycott all Shell products. Picket Shell garages. Do not allow them to profit by their destruction of the people and ecology of the Niger delta...Support the call for a worldwide boycott of Nigerian oil. Help save life and the environment of the Niger delta."[94]

Greenwash is sold by all Transnational Corporations and bought by those not informed on the reality of the damage they create adhering to pre-described lifestyle demands. Aside from DuPont and Shell the list includes, but is not limited to: Mobile Corporation guilty of oil pollution, a biodegradability scam, green collar fraud, and sham recycling. Dow Chemical Company guilty of organochlorine contamination, "product stewardship," avoiding liability, and a producer of dioxin contamination. Solvay & CIE S.A. guilty of myths of incineration, recycling, and export recycling (their idea of recycling waste was sending it abroad.) Monsanto for the use of untested, unsafe chemicals and biotech food. Cargill, ConAgra, and other Agri-business affiliates for its abuse of animals, its mass marketing of bacteria contaminated meats, water pollution, and use of radiation to supposedly increase the safety of meats (this questionable procedure was FDA approved in only a few short weeks). Westinghouse for its reckless approach to Nuclear Power construction. International Paper Company for dioxin pollution and clean technology suppression. Mitsubishi for tropical deforestation. The list goes on and on. The real question is how do these corporations stay in business when blatantly disregarding the lives of those who they are purported to serve? Or, once again the question arises, why do we continue to support corporations that cause us harm?

ADMINISTRATIVE WISDOM?

On August 20, 2001, the article "No Greens Need Apply" in the New York Times reported: "While Congress and the country have been debating high-profile environmental issues, like whether to drill for oil in the Arctic, President Bush has been quietly filling key subcabinet posts with conservative activist and industry lobbyists who have spent their careers criticizing the laws they are now sworn to uphold.

These appointments should dispel any doubts about Mr. Bush's intention to weaken the strong environmental protections he inherited from the Clinton administration. Unlike his father, who reached into academia and even the environmental community for some of his appointments, Mr. Bush seems determined to return to the Reagan era, when ideologues like James Watt ran the interior Department and most of the important regulatory jobs were filled with representatives of the businesses they regulated.

Nowhere is Mr. Bush's strategy clearer than at Interior, the agency most responsible for protecting the country's natural resources. The department's new deputy secretary, J. Steven Griles, was a top lobbyist for the oil, gas, and coal industries, which contributed heavily to Mr. Bush's campaign last year and this year helped shape an energy strategy that would open the public lands to drilling. The new solicitor, William Myers III, was a senior employee of the National Cattlemen's Beef Association and represented the nation's grazing interests in lawsuits challenging federal policies that he will now be required to uphold. Bennett Raley, the new assistant secretary for water and science, is likewise a longtime servant of the big landowning and irrigation interests. Lynn Scarlett, the new assistant secretary for policy, was president of the Reason Foundation, a libertarian think tank opposed in principle to most government regulation. All four have won Senate approval. However, there are others with similar professional or ideological pedigrees that have yet to be approved for jobs that wield great power over day to day policy. Senate environmentalists will want to pay closer attention to these nominees lest they wake up one morning to find a fox in every coop."

"Addiction to me is my dependence and desire for something so much that it interferes with and takes over my daily life."

—Celita, 4 ½ years sober

10

Paradigms and Beliefs

"I have come to understand, probably more times than I would like to admit, that often I am the thing I hate most.
Yet, even with this realization, I often repeat what I have acknowledged as self-destructive.
The enemy is not outside the wall, it built the wall from within using brick upon brick of belief."

—W.L. Houser

As legends and history are told, the victories, the celebrations, the fatted calf or sacrificial lamb are remembered, blocking out the fact that our castle was left to burn with our children trapped in the tower. Bottom line, we have trouble looking behind the images of our minds. Robert Dilts, a genius behind modern Neuro-Linguistic Programming, has shown that we only see a straight line in front of us or behind us. Thus, the first image blocks the rest. And, usually, unless other motivations arise, there is not a conscious effort to investigate behind the front image; our insight is restricted due to the way we perceive, rearrange, then recall experience. This very component of our minds, the ability to analyze, if manipulated in a specific manner, shifts what would be a progressive existence to one fraught with futility. This foundation of futility is built upon our beliefs.

PARADIGM THINKING: THE AMERICAN EXPERIMENT

Dr. Bernie S. Siegel says: "We are addicted to our beliefs and we <u>do</u> act like addicts when someone tries to wrest from us the powerful opium of our dogmas." The belief in democracy as our saving grace is such a dogma. As a whole, most Americans believe that there is no threat of harm for those of democracy. This safety rests in the belief that as Americans we have security, safety, and freedom. But how sound is this belief? Jon Ralston Saul states in *The Unconscious Civilization*: "It could be argued that we are now in the midst of a coup d'etat in slow motion. Democracy is weakening; few people would disagree. Corporatism is strengthening; you only have to look around you. Yet none of us has chosen this route for our society, in spite of which our elite's quite happily continue down it. Mussolini said that 'liberty was all right for cavemen, but civilization meant a progressive diminution in personal freedom.' He had a kind of idiot savant feeling for the twentieth century at its worst."[95]

In science, religion, politics, psychology, and the schooling our children culture plays a huge role. In the fall of 2000 the journal Nature reported that one-third of school children in the United States are not taught evolution. For a period in 1999 Kansas once again outlawed the teaching of evolution. One of the reasons for this blatant gap in our educational system is that some like to blame Darwin and his theory of evolution for moral decline. Regardless of the reason for selective curriculum many are taught sub-standard science if not outright inaccurate information.

As Alexis de Tocueville feared: "The American experiment would result in an egalitarian dismissal of excellence, a mass culture isn't culture at all it is entertainment." As Darwin is dismissed as evil in the same year the hottest brand of clothing for young teens (11-13 year-olds) is a brand name called "porn star." The logo is on a star of these garments for everyone to see and sold at the most fashionable locations for 5th 6th and 7th grade children. These children are taught to fit in; they desire to be part of the crowd: popular, and fashionable. This fashion is part of the entertainment and learned images. Porn star, McDonalds, Wal-mart, and Malls are accommodated yet evolution is boycotted.

The Unconscious Civilization continues: "We suffer from an addictive weakness for large illusions. A weakness for ideology. Power in our civilization is repeatedly tied to the pursuit of all-inclusive truths and utopias. At the time of each obsession we are incapable of recognizing our attitude as either a flight from reality or an embracing of ideology. The unshakable belief that we are on the trail to truth—and therefore to the solution to our problems—prevents us from identifying this obsession as an ideology. The history of this century—demonstrated in part by its unprecedented violence—suggests that our addiction is getting worse.

"We have already swept through the religion of world empires based upon the intrinsic superiority of each nation or race of empire builders, on through Marxism and Fascism, and now we are enthralled by a new all-powerful clockmaker god—the marketplace and his archangel, technology. Trade is the marketplace's miraculous cure for all that ails us. And globalization is the Eden or paradise into which the Just shall be welcomed on Judgment Day. As always with ideologies, the Day of Judgment is imminent and terrifying."[96]

Where fear-based control exists democracy becomes vague failing the people it is meant to protect. Democracy depends on a large middle class who is literate, thinking, decision-making entities with a flexible hierarchy. An ideal culture naturally would focus on our inner lives; however, current circular demise tends to radiate from an endeavor to increase material wealth or the outer life. Many think, as the most educated, powerful and wealthy of all countries in the world, that America is infallible. Most believe that we have all the answers. Yet knowing the answer is never as important as being able to ask the right question. As Gregg Levoy says: "We love the answers and suffer the questions. We worship the flower and ignore the soil. We covet the diamond and overlook the pressure it took to make it."[97] He goes on: "Far from being the transcendent experience we imagine, though, this hero or heroine's journey, this search for what is truest in ourselves, turns out to be largely pick-and-shovel work." 21st Century perception detonates the visual that pick and shovel work is for prisoners. Following the Vietnam Conflict the Communist established re-education camps for people whom the Communist leaders viewed as not aligning with their now reigning doctrine. A media trained perception elicits the same results, but without the bad press.

◆   ◆   ◆

Traditions are very conscious attempts to repeat patterns—good, bad or indifferent. It is from concrete images that tradition is established. If you take a look at the patterns that make up your life, then look at those around you, especially family members, you will see much common ground. Also the story, the tradition, or the pattern accelerates as repeated. Often the power of influence makes a learning curve into something like a dip. As intelligent beings this makes little sense—that is unless looking at how the beliefs build one's reality.

STRATEGIES & BELIEFS

How we move through the world involves abilities built with modalities and sub-modalities. A modality is a 'vision'; its sub-modalities are brightness, clarity size, location, and all characteristics in general. We use all these modalities in specific orders to create a strategy. If we want to experience a rose, we see, smell, and touch it. Strategies are how people sequence internal and external images, sounds and feeling. Strategies make sense of perception, creating belief, behaviors, and thought patterns from data. Effective strategies use the most effective images in the best sequence to achieve a particular goal.[98]

While strategies are how experience is organized, beliefs are the core motivation behind behavior. We all have beliefs about a multitude of things. Some beliefs can be traced back to their source, while others have vague origins. Listening to how we explain our position can identify beliefs. If there are words such as 'should' or 'should not', 'ought' or 'ought not,' 'can' or 'can't' there is probably a belief in place feeding this particular perception and ultimately the behavior. Jack's dominant belief was that he was a slick business guy, this belief, this image of himself blocked all other components such as the consequences of his addiction. My friends believe that $1,000,000 will bring them happiness, never looking behind this image for other inroads to peace. They also do not review the pressure they place on themselves with work or the fact that their bickering just may be due to this stress.

Beliefs often do not live up to sensory-based reality checks. We might believe that $1,000,000 would make us happy, yet how often have we heard that this amount of money did not bring relief. But because beliefs are higher patterned with some lasting a lifetime[99] such beliefs that money brings happiness is so woven into our psyche that it is difficult to doubt or question it until we personally earn that million and are still quite miserable. Unfortunately most don't make it that far and die in process or make it over and over but compulsively spend it before the math can be done to prove its presence.

Beliefs also tend to have some consistency. When we look at our beliefs there probably will surface specific patterns, sounds, and pictures. Because of those trillion bits of incoming data sometimes it is hard to establish if the belief was created with reality based imagery or fantasy based imagery. Did we watch a movie when we were young where the rich people were the happy ones? Did JR and the Ewing power captivate us before entering kindergarten? Can we remember why it is so important that we behave in a certain manner? Sit like a lady, or act like a man? Why we respond vehemently to certain prompts but are able to forgive other abuses that are much more foul? Understanding our belief systems are important because there are beliefs that keep us stuck and beliefs that propel us forward. Which belief does what and why usually takes focused investigation.

There also exist belief strategies, which is the way we maintain and protect beliefs. These belief strategies also work automatically. In addiction, as we have seen, we call these strategies rationalizations and justifications. When the strategy is doing its job it blinds one to the consequences that sprout up as a result of certain beliefs, even though these consequences actually are what eventually clarifies what beliefs, habits, lifestyles, and patterns are working against us. We all do a degree of rationalizing instinctively to defend comfort levels be it in the form of brain chatter or an outright oral defense. All addicts are experts at rationalizing their addiction as well as the corresponding chaotic consequences. Jack with his bandaged hands or Ray with his new economy have clear belief systems feeding the path of their lives. Jack's belief, colored by his addictive mentality, conveyed that the burns were simply an error in judgment. Ray used the old adage of survival of the fittest not realizing that as humans the waters of progression would hopefully run much deeper.

Like Ray's rationale or cheesecake as a health food, often belief strategies make little sense when investigated. Ray's belief was a defense built on a childhood riddled with poverty and hunger where he watched the drug dealers in his inner city neighborhood prosper. His belief system grew from the distorted chain of events he experienced. His prosperity became his defense, his image protecting him from his core fears. His belief strategy, survival at all costs, is a type of offensive assemblage; a wall hiding what would eventually destroy him. Yet because of his experience, though his pattern destructive, it resides in a comfort level. He not only knew the game; he was used to it. These comfort levels make it difficult to change even though the real experience of blistered hands or excessive jail time is present.

Real experience is coded different than a strategy contrived on beliefs. When perception is built on clear, concrete experience reality strategies emerge. Reality strategies are how we validate our experience.

If we hit our hand with a hammer, it hurts. If we overeat, we gain weight. If we break the law, we go to jail. In the same arena, reality strategies would stand up in court; belief strategies usually would not.

Unlike the imbalance of some beliefs and their individualized influence, reality strategies are the way that you can determine precisely how you need to think to be convinced that something is legitimate enough for you to do.[100] Concrete data with proven results are what reality strategies are made of. Reality strategies encompass both the good and bad. For addicts, it is usually the loss of everything. They rarely see the need to alter their behavior until a lot of consequences hit home. Sometimes this is a heart attack from use, overwhelming stress, or legal issues. Other times it is simply the inability to afford their habit. Regardless of the specific instigator, at some point reality based circumstances overwhelm the sugarcoated beliefs ushering in reality's change.

ANCHORS

The process of self-talk, from beginning to end, feeds confusion due to the subliminal imprints and anchors of the mind. Imprints are events from our past, which ignites the formation of a belief or several beliefs. The experience or imprint is not the issue; it is the impression that is left behind. This impression is known as an anchor. The feel good sensation, the anchor, was imprinted by the first use of crack for Jack. The belief instilled with this experience created a more powerful anchor than the reality of the bandages for Jack. For Ray, the imprint of security and power that his money gave him was the anchor that fed continuing in his profession even in light of potential, severe jail time.

Anchoring is the process of associating internal emotional responses with external stimuli. Anchors are like triggers except they are deeper; they actually feed motivation because they support beliefs. Anchors are why we believe as we believe in certain situations. Jack built the belief that he was a successful businessman on the imprint of his real estate transactions. Even though the evolution of his business dealings took a turn, the core belief remained a huge motivation. Thus, the anchor—business transactions in general—elicited feelings of success even though Jack's life, due to his addiction, had become the polar opposite.

From the time we are born anchors are created. Anchors can be helpful or debilitating. Experiences from childhood have imprints and anchors that still initiate feelings as an adult. Anchors can lead to positive beliefs that are useful or negative beliefs that can be limiting. A powerful anchor is dependency. From infant dependency on a parent forward, dependency is a seed that lies within us all. Aside from brain chemistry, as humans we have a natural affiliation to addictive behaviors because of this dependency. Depending on the imprint and the belief that has evolved, a degree of dependency is continually played out in our lives.

Often the anchors that exist in our lives hold the reasoning behind what appears as poor choice; they show these poor choices are really subliminally sparked compulsions. Anchors happen as quickly as chemical triggers and usually are someone else's ideas transplanted into the psyche; thus, anchors result in the manifestation of specific behaviors ignited by implanted images. Anchors are another reason why propaganda and commercials work.

SCRIPTS, SCHEMAS, AND ARCHETYPES

A series of anchors and beliefs could be considered a script or schema. Scripts are decisions we make about life at an early age in regards to our self and others. We also use schemas, which are a system of core beliefs on how the world works: i.e. if it is bad or good, happy or sad or if it is threatening or kind. Schemas, scripts, and belief systems repeat themselves generation after generation in a subconscious manner; thus, creating archetypes. Archetypes are important because they recreate patterns at subconscious and generational levels.

The image of King Solomon is an archetype, so is the devil. Fearing hell is a belief system that evolves from archetypal religious dogma. Mother Nature is an archetype with a series of beliefs that correspond with what she represents. Our forefathers and their idea of a republic, which has evolved into what we commonly call democracy, is another archetype. Believing the idea that regulators protect us from environmental poisons is a belief system built on idealistic archetypes. Archetypes are primitive images that are building blocks of the collective conscious. They are inherited ideas that get passed along at what seems to be a cellular level.

Freud talked about archetypes saying that all we do is derived from archetypes and sexual energy, which is driven by the id, ego, or superego. The 'Id' is core sexual and aggressive energy. The Id is also where desire resides. It is here that core, unrestrained energy can cause havoc. It is what is active at birth and if not developed continues to rule the person.

As we mature we shift from these inner impulses allowing our mind to mediate external reality, allowing us to question the automatic responses that often rule our days and nights. Yet, when bombarded with images, which ignite anchors with their corresponding cravings and patterns there is little time to reevaluate the details that make up lifestyle so instantaneously.

PROPAGANDA: A POWERFUL SUB-MODALITY

When what is innately known as truth gets contaminated with someone else's brand of truth, usually someone selling something, the prospect of propaganda enters the game of beliefs and reality. Propaganda is someone trying to inflict his or her brand of truth on another to create a specific behavior. It is the installation of certain beliefs to incite responses. Propaganda is one of the most powerful sub-modalities in existence in this media driven age. Propaganda is perpetuated by the use of movies, images, and sounds that feed certain contrived belief strategies.

A main strength of propaganda is that it tells us what we want to hear in a way that ignites comfort. After planting seeds that lead to various beliefs with corresponding cravings, it also initiates belief strategies that pacify, anesthetize, or placate conflicting data. Propaganda not only creates and instills specific comfort zones; it builds the wall that will defend these comfort levels should questions arise. Comfort levels are powerful; people do not tend to leave their comfort zone until discomfort is great. This occurs regardless of the corresponding reality created by belief and lifestyle habits. Instilling beliefs in the sovereign people of a nation is very different than the various freedoms America is said to have been founded. Propaganda to a democracy is like alcohol to a drunk. Propaganda goes back as far as man. Though it existed before Constantine, his life is an excellent example.

Constantine, in the 4th Century had his own propagandist, Eusebius, who wrote in such a way as to make Constantine seem god-like. Eusebius describing Constantine: "In short, as the sun, when he rises upon the earth, liberally imparts his rays of light to all, so did Constantine, proceeding at early dawn from the imperial palace and rising as it were with the heavenly luminary, impart the rays of his own beneficence to all who came into his presence."[101] This type of propaganda fed Constantine's power and claim to fame, which include taking the cross from a method of capital punishment to a symbol of Christianity.

As his propaganda progressed, ruled by his perception of dominance, the specifics of Christianity would begin their long journey into distortion. Yet, Constantine's ego and arrogance were a most powerful perpetrator; his sword was the cross; his intent was the unification of a very diverse, conflicted Roman Empire. Unfortunately the result was more of a totalitarian regime than one based on humanity. Knowing the game of propaganda has written a clear role in history for Constantine.

More recently, the use of propaganda to unite can be seen in the origination of Thanksgiving Day in 1863. Patriotism needed a boost so Lincoln felt such a holiday could pull people together for the right reasons; and it did. During this period people were known to print the speeches of the day and meet to discuss them. Voting was at an all time high. But this does not obscure propaganda's dark side.

The use of propaganda became more obvious in the early 1900's. The U.S. government needed to get some energy moving due to the war across the ocean. We were a pacifist populous and President Wilson thought we should be in the war; so he set out to motivate his people. He created the Creel Commission to bombard the public with propaganda that not only had Americans asking to go to war in six months, but also had Americans wanting to destroy anything of German heritage. This was the shift from covert to overt manipulation with propaganda.

Propaganda worked so well it was used over and over again. The Red Scare was next;[102] it included twenty-eight African Americans being burned alive, hundreds of union activists deported, and tens of thousands of people blacklisted.[103] Propaganda was used to destroy unions and free press. Hitler did it in Germany.[104] Today the destruction of free speech due to government control happens more then anyone would ever care to admit. And where a gag-policy exists, where freedom of speech is muzzled; propaganda is always present to fill in the gaps.

Propaganda is very subtle; it plays into the beliefs of a particular culture then often builds a type of self-righteous positioning on a particular belief. We see this in the Middle East as 'religious-based' tapes are distributed to a mostly illiterate population to train their minds toward the cause (usually anti-west or anti-American). These tapes teach the listener to go into the streets and scream 'Infidel!' 'Infidel!' at passing Americans. These tapes manipulate a pacifist into a rebel, then a rebel into a killer.

On a societal scale this manipulation happens in revolutionary form, with many faces. Walter Lippmann saw a "revolution in the art of democracy" that could be used to "manufacture consent." Noam Chomsky notes our alignment as the 'bewildered herd,' which insinuates a mass brainwashing. Propaganda, used to brainwash at societal level involves a shift in core instinct. Instinct is modified or conditioned to gravitate towards a particular mode of behavior instantly. Aristotle referred to it as 'right thinking.' Hitler referred to it as 'the Master Race.' Or, more blatantly, The Creel Commission identified that propaganda could be used to convince people to agree to things they didn't want (like war)—'to control the public mind.' [105]

Current day media refers to it as 'meeting consumer demand.' Bush masks his ecological war as "Compassionate Conservatism." Monsanto just wants to "feed the world." Mobile only shoots for "Target: environmental excellence." Dow is only "Developing environmental solutions that make a world of difference." Shell is just "Caring for the world." General Motors is into something called "Geo-logic." In today's society there exists an endless array of leaders, manipulators, and outright liars with personal hierarchies in mind for others willing to use their slant to make money. Propaganda in Western Culture is that of the eternal sell or communal greenwash. Naturally a residual of a population who is busy spending is a population who is also busy working. When busy trying to survive it is difficult to keep up with all that is going on then compare notes and realize all the distortions. Propaganda is not only a powerful tool; it is a lethal distortion of reality; and the Achilles Heel to modern democracy.

PRE-PROGRAMMED ACCEPTANCE

Morris Berman states in *The Twilight of American Culture* that 70% of Americans believe in angels, 50% of us believe in UFO's, and 30% believe they have made contact with the dead.[106] Pandora's box is open. The human psyche goes daily on the auction block to the highest bidder. Our attention distracted by more and more absurd deceptions. Addiction swims in the waters of deception, like a shark, it dominates in a most malignant, abstruse way. But again, because of distraction, we don't realize its presence until we're missing body parts.

McDonalds, Burger King, Kellogg, Honda, Chevy, Ajax, Tide, Keebler, Nike, Campbells, Ford, Microsoft, AT&T or whoever is doing the advertising, plants a subtle anchor into our psyches. Disney would be amazed at how his seedlings have grown: igniting cravings, images seen, key phrase heard, then sensory experience automatically overrides conscious thought. Like the SUV and the Hummer, there are more feeds than I can mention. 'Just Do It,' 'Buy Brennan,' 'Like a Rock' all immediately initiate a feeling from the imagery imprinted by commercials. 'You deserve a break today,' sound familiar? *Culture Jam* states that Americans recognize fewer than ten plants but recognize one thousand corporate logos. We have cravings for things we can identify and cravings for things we can not. We have difficulty pulling away from the subliminal feeds of whoever owns the time frame even though it is someone else's ideas going straight into the cells of our brains.

We believe our consumption is normal because it is all we have known. Since a very young age we experienced happiness from the front of a shopping cart; an imprint occurred. Then the anchor of feeling good while shopping initiates happiness. We form the belief that consumerism, shopping, and excess is a good part of the American lifestyle. Beliefs are fed with mass media's depiction of what a healthy economy is, an economy is a place where productivity is always increasing. Yet this type of productivity is an obvious lie, at some point productivity levels out. It has to; the world that provides the raw materials is only so big.

Ultimately, propaganda is no different than drug dealing, except we are taught to accept it and the consumption it ignites as normal even though this is done by the very influence of the advertisements and propaganda that ignited the trigger/anchor in the first place. Worse yet we defend the repercussions such as pollution, global warming, obesity, starvation, and social imbalance as acceptable fallout to the Western way of life. This is mainly because the very imprints that came from the original propaganda have been a large contributor to a belief system that rationalizes no responsibility as an acceptable stance.

The cycle of influence based on imprints, anchors, and beliefs is illogical to someone of a different belief system, someone on the outside looking in. Often, when I worked with an addict's family they continually reiterated their confusion at the addict's patterns, rationalizations, and continued behavior in light of consequences. From their position they could easily see the insanity. Other countries criticize the US for many of the patterns it propagates, especially its wasteful nature. From their position, again the outside looking in, they can see the insanity and often, like an addict's circle of family and friends, experience some of addictions' consequences.

◆   ◆   ◆

Confusion between fantasy images and real images affect many spiritually and emotionally. We mistake intensity for depth, joy and love losing objectivity and our sense of balance. In seeking the 'good-life' we compromise ourselves. The 'good-life' won't make us happy because, again, we are using something outside of ourselves to fill a void that is within and keeps resurfacing. There is conflict between our belief and reality strategies.[107] We are predators, who seek the sensation of pleasure to avoid feelings, which continues to move us deeper into addiction.

The alcoholic or addict, due to their disease, and by the obscure relationship that continues between their personal emotions and blind instinctual sensations are unable and prevented from experiencing the confrontation of the basic forces within themselves. Thus, in addiction, by default, survival rationalized instinct will seek to accommodate impulsive craving every notch up the ladder of consumption. Archetypes feed scripts, schemas, and beliefs as scripts, schemas and beliefs feed archetypes. This vicious cycle is one of the reasons we keep doing the same things over and over explaining the dip that history has documented.

" I thought everyone drank like I did. It was my normal, so it was everyone else's normal too."

—Karen 6 months sober

11

Dissonance

"Just as the hand, held before the eyes, hides the tallest mountain, so does our ordinary way of seeing hide the many wonders of which the world is full."

—Dr. Jack Vallentyne

When self-image or self-esteem are threatened, as we have seen, we become rationalizing animals rather than question beliefs. Leon Festinger, a social psychologist who authored a theory on cognitive dissonance, describes and predicts how we rationalize behaviors. This theory is one step beyond that 'why' to the perception screen through which we view the world. Culture, traditions, scripts, beliefs, and archetypes create the screen; strategies protect it; and cognitive dissonance defends it. Thus, in order to place doubt in those core beliefs, not only must we identify the belief, but also the defense that is a shield around it. It is this defense shield that makes sense of two conflicting beliefs or opinions. This state of conflict is uncomfortable and at some point either something must give in a major way or new rationalizations must be formed. Depending on what is at stake people will go to great lengths of distortion, denial and self-persuasion in order to justify past or current behavior & beliefs.

Images fed by propaganda, intentionally arouse feelings of dissonance by threatening self-esteem due to guilt trips related to images that are tough to live up to: The perfect body, look or car. But then a solution is offered to reduce the dissonance: buy this machine, that car or vote this way and you'll feel better.[108] Seems like a trap because it is.

It has a direct effect on the development and maintenance of addiction. It is a major component that sways the dynamics of who we try to be by setting up a strategy that is hard to resist, that ultimately appeases fear and scarcity, but just for a minute.

A TRIP TO CLARION?

Marian Keech was a middle-aged woman who lived in the Midwest in the early 1950s and claimed to receive messages from outer space. Marian also had a following of a small but faithful clan. On one clear evening in September she received a message from the planet Clarion telling her that on December 21 the world would be destroyed by a great flood. This message also said their fleet of saucers would rescue her. This is when Marian put the word out and managed to gain her loyal group of followers. These followers quit their jobs, gave away their money, houses, possessions, and withdrew from their friends. Some even left their spouses. A few social psychologists intentionally became a part of the group so they could watch the process of the group when the ships did not arrive from Clarion.

On the morning of December 20th Marian received a message from Clarion as to what she and her followers needed to do to prepare for their trip. It instructed them to make sure all metal was off their clothing, which included zippers, snaps, and clasps. Thus the group dutifully removed all items and awaited their pick up at midnight. By four A.M. the group sat in stunned silence—some doubt had to be surfacing. But at four forty-five Marian got another message. This message said that the world was being spared of cataclysm. The flood was off because of the wonderful faith of this small group. Apparently this small group who had sat all night had spread enough love that the God of Earth had changed his mind. The group was relieved and happy about the change in plans. At this point you'd think the reality of their absurd beliefs would sink in and they would bail.

However, interestingly enough, within twenty-four hours this shy-reclusive bunch called newspapers and TV stations so they could talk about their prophecy and why it had failed or was successful, depending on your point of reference. These people made speeches, stood on street corners handing out leaflets, and tried to attract more followers in general. There was a new urgency in spreading their message. The question the social psychologists asked was 'why?' Remember, these people had given up everything for their flight to Clarion; thus it was easier for them to maintain a deluded belief system than take the hit to their self-image that reality would introduce. Thus, they made the lie grow, defending it even more. And what is the best way to defend a lie? By convincing others of course! If they could persuade others that their beliefs had saved the world they had not sacrificed their lives in vain and would not have to face the enormity of their mistake. Convincing others would allay their doubts. Through this whole process they went from believers to zealots.[109]

What made Marion want to go to a different planet? Was she simply a bit touched or had something triggered a deep desire within her to escape? How did she influence others to join her? What seed did she trigger that enabled her to integrate and replace her model of the world over theirs? The people who chose to follow Marion had something missing in their lives. There was some type of doubt present that allowed the integration of different beliefs and a new lifestyle. They must have sensed that there is something more, in search for an answer, they joined Marion's group. Though Marion's model was eccentric, it worked for her followers and her. And, it is an extreme demonstration of how not only specific models of the world are created, but also how they are protected.

◆   ◆   ◆

Whether bowing to the belief structures of a neighborhood or a cult leader or a country there is a spectrum of structure that is delicate. As structure evolves there is a place where it can become slanted by control. The same happens in judgment. There is a line where judgment becomes criticism. There is a line where expectations turn dark and morph into manipulation and where freethinking becomes robotic. There is a line where traditional beliefs turn into apathy. There is a place that elicits transparency but turns into walls. And, there is a line where social conditioning is control—this is when lifestyle becomes addiction. Subtlety is everything. Where the line between potentiality is shifted from an evolution of goodness to an evolution of greed is hard to pin down; but it is there and there are consequences to an evolution that does not embrace the bettering of *all life*. The bettering of life entertains a search for truth. Yet again, mental pollution and the emotional sabotage of the pyramid power structure stagnate this process.

DUMBING US DOWN

While the corporate and political world take advantage of the media, using it to influence, some, like Joseph Chilton Pearce, see it as an actual reversal in the evolutionary process of the human race; a 'dumbing down' that we see the results of in our crime statistics and that could ultimately result in the disintegration of human society.[110]

In the book *Dumbing Us Down* John Gatto, a New York school teacher, clearly shows that the policy and techniques of the public school system promote a manner of education that is more conducive of corporate drones than analytical, intelligent individualists. In the Food and Water Journal Camy Matthay describes: "Schools have always supported societies based on hierarchies of privilege and power. In America, the whole notion of social mobility through education is flawed; it is here that revolutionary consciousness has foundered on the unexamined assumption of upward mobility—the very fabric of the American Dream.

"When ambition no longer seeks competence, when moving up appears as the only prize worth pursuing, one is more likely to end up chained to the convention that money is an adequate goal for life's work, than involved in redefining the American Dream, much less working to confront injustice and the hierarchy of privilege and power in America. Not withstanding my recognition that we are all embedded in a particular society on a particular course, I hope that my own children understand my dissent with mainstream culture. If I am able to instill in them objectivity about the hurricane of false meaning produced in our society, I believe that their capacity to think for and believe in themselves will not be as foreshortened as mine was by the years I spent in school.

"My greatest longing is for my children to retain clarity of mind, to conduct their lives with compassion for others, and to understand the worth of working to create self-sustaining, self-governing communities. I would like them to be more useful than important and to know and exalt the authentic forms of happiness that can't be bought. I want them to be capable of sober thoughts and the action that clarifies what is fair and true."[111]

◆   ◆   ◆

The realization that the seeds of many lives have been grown from someone else's thoughts, fed by 'techno' inputs, and ultimately become lifestyle by faceless masters of manipulation is not on any billboard, commercial or warning label. Somewhere along the yellow brick road of progress many get lost in a designer inflated illusion. This pressure is not only enormous; it is generally unnoticed. A type of secrecy is maintained because, like evolution, awareness of addiction threatens the oppressive power of secular faith and industry. Confronting addiction affects the ability of certain entities to shape culture because it confronts the oppression that society accepts as normal.

"Addicts are always talking about this is the last time, making up excuses, but never follow up with action.
We just keep going on with our craziness until we are knocked down hard enough to sit and think."

—Anonymous

PART IV
The Roots of Oppression

o o o o o o o o o o o o o o o o o o o o o o o o o o o o o o o o o

"Embellished by promises of limitless and effortless afflu-
ence, the vision of a global economy has an entrancing
appeal.

Beneath its beguiling surface, however, we find a modern
form of enchantment, a siren song created by the skilled
image makers of Madison Avenue, enticing societies to
weaken community to free the market, eliminate livelihoods
to create wealth, and destroy life to increase unneeded and
often unsatisfying consumption."

—*When Corporations Rule the World*
David Korten

12

The Seeds of Oppression

"Perfection's of means and confusion of goals seem—in my opinion—to characterize our age."

—Albert Einstein

Abigail Adams confronted her husband on the double standards of 1774 asking: "fight ourselves for what we are daily robbing and plundering from those who have as good a right to freedom as we have." As an indirect response concerning slavery Patrick Henry's excuse entailed: "I am drawn along by the general inconvenience of living here without them."[112] We still use that one, just in a different context.

OPPRESSION

Oppression has subtly woven a clear path throughout history. Many of our ancestors began their stay in America as indentured servants or slaves, which entailed clearing forests, building roads, farmsteads, and forts for trading posts. If these indentured servants did this for seven years they were then given the opportunity to lease a parcel of land. The lucky servants who lived past the seven years (and many did not) could become rentersto wealthy landowners such as George Washington, Thomas Jefferson, James Madison and Ben Franklin.[113]

Many Americans like believing that we began as a united people, which to some extent is true compared to what the Protestant Church pulled off in the motherland of England there was opportunity in this new America for most citizens. In 1517 in England when the Protestant Church took over from the Catholics they drove the poor farmers off the land for the nobles. These poor farmers were without a place to live; thus, they were branded, punished, jailed, or sold into slavery.[114] (Didn't New York do something similar to the homeless recently?) Seven years as an indentured servant, even with the high death rate, probably seemed reasonable.

The slave trade was also going on at this time. (This first attempt at globalization included all the abuse of the Third World countries that it does today.) The slave trade spanned three centuries and relocated ten to twelve million Africans.[115] Servants or slaves, bought and sold, there existed a lot of persuaded volunteers and it was time to build a nation. At the time of the War for Independence three out of four persons in Virginia, Maryland and Pennsylvania were or had been indentured servants and 20% were slaves.[116] (Thomas Jefferson wrote that everyone had the right to: "Life, liberty, and the pursuit of happiness." At the time of his death he owned 267 slaves, he set 8 free, which happened to be his relatives.[117])

Next came the development firms. These speculators got the profits. They set up such enterprises as the Ohio Company in 1748, which was organized by Lawrence Washington (George's brother). Lawrence got a grant of 200,000 acres of land west of Virginia from the King of England and ships' passage for indentured servants. Between the free land and free help, business was booming. (Isn't there something like this going on in India and Columbia with peasants? Thailand and Mexico with farmers? China with prisoners? S. Dakota with Native Americans?) The other competition was the Loyal Land Company of Virginia, which Thomas Jefferson's father was part owner, and the Vandalia Company, which was partly owned by Ben Franklin.[118]

THE RE-BIRTH OF CORPORATE POWER

The Revolutionary War was fought for many reasons, but primarily it was due to the exploitation of the settlers with imbalances in taxation.

This exploitation of the new colonies was done by the British Crowns' monopolies: The British East India Company and The Hudson Bay Company. This conflict became the motivation that propelled The Revolutionary War forward. These monopolies formed specifically to exploit the colonies and control their markets.[119] With the war over, the intimidating power of corporate entities dominated the memory of the Founding Fathers, as did the reality that tables can turn quickly. Thus, they looked at corporations as a necessary evil to be highly regulated by government and watched carefully by citizen organizations.

Corporations originally were for special circumstances only, such as public purposes and short-term projects verses long-term endeavors. Corporations and business were separate under the law of the land, which instigated a great level of control over business and corporations both. In business there was a person who had to adhere to the law. But as the country grew so did business. Business became a very different force, with a vital shift in its core philosophy. The American eagle was traded for a vulture as far as corporations go—and the vultures were circling.

The weak spot then emerged, a time of perfected vulnerability. After the Civil War, with a torn country, the assassination of President Lincoln, corruption, disruption, and a political fog as thick as smoke the final shift began. With Grant as president, having both alcohol and war stealing his best years, a sinister era of politics set to free corporations of the restraints that so wisely were in place. In 1886 with the decision of the Supreme Court in the Santa Clara County v. Southern Pacific Railroad, corporations began enjoying the full rights of citizens while not having to adhere to the responsibilities and liabilities of individual citizens.[120]

Since 1896, just a short decade after the landmark Santa Clara County case, corporations proved their ability to grow enormously, become powerful entities, and to make massive amounts of money.[121] They have proven over and over that our forefather's were wise in demanding strict regulation. The abuse of power through money, bribes, and lobbyists has become flamboyantly obvious. From 1997 to 1999 lobbyists grew 37% to 20,000 and spent $1.42 billion persuading our congressmen—that's 38 lobbyists for each congressman.[122] The lack of separation of corporation and government has shown to be something of a monster. The Food &Water Journal states, "In truth, the law of real people can no longer direct corporate actions. That is to say, corporations govern. Like Dr. Frankenstein's monster, the creation is now the master of the creator."[123]

With the rise of production, regulations, electronics, lobbyists, chemicals, energy use, and automation, the corporation grew with advertising as its right hand helper, then grew some more; then began to merge. From Monsanto to Union Carbide to Cargill to Microsoft we have before us dealers of enormous proportion—to the tune of trillions. As corporations made more money their power further penetrated government. Ego-based control grew. Money moved markets, barriers, politics and worlds. For we as consumers, there was never a place where there was enough.

As TV sways consumers, the world is thrown into new motion. What was meant to bring more to those who had less, began to simply bring more to those who have more and show many all they did not have. An addiction to things was given a major shot in the arm. Here is where tradition took a turn. Here is where our culture could be spoon fed propaganda and shaped accordingly. Here is where we began to talk less to each other and more to a box. Here is a beginning of the numbing of our senses. Oppression is easier to tolerate if there is good TV.

Various triggers, images, and anchors are well in place. The pleasure god found, many simply buy, over and over; repetition without thought has become the norm. There is always that new style, the latest model car, a bigger house, a better way, the latest, newest, biggest, more and more, on and on. Habit without conscience infiltrated all levels of existence. Fed by a tradition of 'needing more,' inflated images became power.

◆   ◆   ◆

The reality that many of our ancestors were in the line for 'branding' but escaped by way of ship to America are the roots to segregation. Segregation in many degrees has always been a dominant color of any organized society. Today the colors of segregation can be seen in the factory workers, corporate drones, fast food workers, or many of the low paying, dependent positions that the worker bees of society struggle with. The lines between fear and desire have grown together. Negativity surfaces in the confusion.

How long can we tolerate a sense of self that is dictated by one or two word phrases? How long will we leave our thinking to others whose thinking has turned on us? As we reach for more and more doesn't it seem we are settling for less? Good intentions are drowning in a flood of products that we have difficulty resisting. Then, at some point, the void can no longer be medicated; the pain resurfaces with new fury. In addiction one cannot hide from their own negative thinking, which evolves from the pursuit of more, draining energy, ultimately this negativity blocks the path to our higher self.

And, where there is an absence of a dominant inner design, where desire is inescapable, and where there is a mass manipulation of the mind, it is inevitable that the inner wish to understand becomes seized by greed. Buried in 'shoulds,' human vices take hold. These vices are powered by a lower function trying to imitate the undeveloped higher self. This is not just a force; it is an innate energy. If this energy is blocked it is redistributed somehow.[124] When one no longer tries to understand all that is placed before them, they end up trying to control it. And where there is no longer the need to understand, where control exists, fear dominates.

"I don't know how I got here, I'm not even sure why I am here.
I know you told me I was arrested for drunk driving with my kids
in the car, but who brought me here? I think jail would be easier.
I don't know if I can do this, I am not even sure I want to.
You said I am here to stop drinking? Your nuts, I can't live with-
out drinking.
This whole thing is really starting to piss me off. I want to see my
kids.
Did you say you knew where they are? I feel like shit."

—Anonymous, one day sober in medical detox, the police
brought her in after she was found unconscious behind the wheel
of her car at a stop light with her three children ages: 4, 6, 7. She
eventually stayed sober.

13

The Happy Global Village

VLADIMIR. *This is getting really insignificant.*
ESTRAGON. *Not Enough.*

—*Waiting for Godot*, Samuel Beckett

We own stock to make money, build security, and maybe even get lucky and strike it rich. This is the way of the market; the way of the world; and, the way of progress. Stockholders expect performance from the companies they invest in. Productivity is God. AT&T is a great example of this. Their chairman, Armstrong, had a vision; the vision was to be able to offer integrated, interconnected services. But his vision needed not only money but also stockholder patience.

Vision was and is expensive for AT&T. In the end billions in revenue and profits are fine, but the market isn't impressed if you have to spend a lot to get there. Even though their integrated vision would be more productive, hold more integrity, and work better for investors in the long run in the immediate this meant less; instant gratification was put on hold for many. Thus, AT&T stock price plummeted 50% from $55.00 a share to $29.00 in a year. Armstrong was eventually ousted, and a guy named Malone was hired to rev up their PR.

For stocks to continue to manifest earnings they must not only decrease the cost of production, but forfeit vision. This is costly to everyone. To increase productivity, industry must close down its expensive American factories and take their production abroad where they can pay two dollars an hour versus a working American wage that exists for their expensive American workers. The stockholders get their dividends, but are now laid off, so they must cash in their stock to survive. Everyone loses in this cycle of consume, produce, perform, and endless profit. Yet, The New World Order has been established. It is presented as the model society.

THE NEW WORLD ORDER

The New World Order is this century's definition of progress, sort of industry's contribution to evolution—a marketing system based in fear. As every life form is engaged in a struggle for existence, life in the Global Village is an existence where money equates wellness. We are sold that The New World Order is the obvious evolution of our economy. Yet it is big business, big money, and a prime example of the pyramid system.

Corporations run the Happy Global Village and are said to serve the public in many ways. They provide jobs for laborers and products for consumers. But most importantly, they make a lot of money. It is propagated that corporations work closely with government and politicians in the best interest of 'we the people.' Politicians, regulatory agencies, CEOs, and the World Bank all work together. They also work with those who facilitate trade: GATT, NAFTA, and the WTO.

The WTO is free trade; free trade is neo-libertarianism. Free trade and its form of libertarianism are said to be good; it opens up markets, bringing more goods and services to those who reside in the Third World, and most importantly, bringing everyone closer to democracy. Free trade simplifies international transactions improving the lives of many. The global village is believed to be a happy one. It operates on a simple premise: increase consumerism, so production needs to be increased, then there will be more jobs for those poor, dense souls who were once self-sufficient but were run off their land to build the toxic, waste laden factory.

Regardless of fallout, globalization is said to be good; it is the new culture. Free trade, globalization, the new economic order, and the happy global village also make a lot of money. Those at the helm of this pursuit are powerful; they own a quarter of the productive assets of the world, this is the culmination of around 300 firm's assets put together.[125] There are 358 billionaires in the world worth $760 billion—which is equal to the worth of 2.5 billion of the world's poorest people.[126] It appears to me that the simple inequality of money here dictates that this cartel is not the ideal group to bring fairness to the world. I would think their understanding of baselines would be a bit off.

THE RICH

The rich are different, and always have been—at least that is what they would have us believe. Corporate CEO's are of the very rich. Their world is different. But they have their struggles too. In 1993 a Forbes magazine article discussed the 400 richest people in America. It conveyed the idea that it had become a struggle for them to make ends meet. This struggle was due to the fact that in one year the price of a one-kilo tin of beluga malossol caviar had increased by 28% to $1408. There also was an 8% increase in a Sikorsky S-780 helicopter to a cool $7 million. And the price to stay over night in New York, in the fashion they have become accustomed to, had increased 15 % to $750 a night.[127]

If this is a struggle to them, they would have real trouble with the budget constraints of a peasant. Their idea of sacrifice falls on others. The corporate libertarians clearly state: "Mexican workers, including children, are heroes of the new economic order...sacrificing their health, lives, and futures on the altar of global competition."[128] These Mexicans live on the U.S./Mexican border and work in U.S. factories known as Maquiladora plants. It is these people which libertarians dub heroes.

This 'free trade' world houses its hundreds of thousands of workers in miles of shanty towns. The towns are made of scrap metal with no sewage systems. They drink from barrels that gather rainfall—barrels that once held toxic chemicals. The workers earn $1.64 an hour though their US counterparts earn an average of $16.17 an hour.[129] They are brutalized or killed if they do not behave. Industrial solvents dumped in the water (levels up to 50,000ppm more than U.S. allows) cause babies to be born without brains.[130] The title 'Heroic' may fit, but it is not by choice. Rather the border people are sacrifices; trying to survive in the New World order with peasant backgrounds. They are victims of the latest definition of progress.

BUILDING MISGUIDED BELIEFS AND BUDGETS

John Galbraith states in *The Affluent Society*: "Economic society was an arena in which men met to compete. The market established the terms of the struggle. Those who won were rewarded with survival and, if they survived brilliantly, with riches. Those who lost went to the lions. This competition not only selected the strong but also developed their faculties and ensured their perpetuation. And in eliminating the weak, it ensured that they would not reproduce their kind. Thus the struggle was socially benign and, to a point at least merciless, the more benign it effects, for the more weaklings it combed out."[131]

Moving money and markets is an unfeeling task. Yet, it is numbers that tell us if we are good and as capitalists we like to measure our capitalistic ways, so we can see how good we are. Adding up all the goods and services is called a GDP or Gross Domestic Product. Once all these goods and services come together and are made one, that one, the GDP, is our measuring stick; thus, making it good or look good is a priority.

If I buy a car, it is a plus for the GDP. When I trash that car it is a plus for the GDP. The service of making that car go away, the service of getting rid of the material in the car, the service of storing its toxic parts, the service of recycling parts of it, and if I am injured, the service of fixing me are all a plus for the GDP. The same goes for TVs, appliances, clothes, bottled water, and much more. My consumeristic ways are good for the GDP. If I were a wasteful consumer I would be good for the GDP. A lot of wasteful consumers make the GDP skyrocket. And a skyrocketing GDP says we as a country are good. This is an example of measuring our wellness with money. We in the U.S. appear to be doing really, really well—but appearances can be deceiving. In all reality the minus sign does exist, whether we acknowledge its presence or not.

In our proposed wellness we also count things such as costs of divorce lawyers due to families breaking apart or security systems due to increased crime. We even count the cost to clean up oil spills, toxic dump sites, radioactive waste removal,[132] and all the medical costs for the folks that were living near these and didn't know they were beginning to glow. Though these are bad we count them as good. We should have good numbers for a long time.

Destroying nature is also good for the GDP (at least in the short term). Destroying it is big business. Cleaning up oil, toxic, and chemical spills or radioactivity is big business—risky, but big. However, the damage to the environment after it has been stripped, cut, burned, or spilled upon is not counted as a minus to the GDP because it is big business that leaves the mess. This is where those minus signs haunt us.

Yet, countries are businesses, their assets and budgets compare to corporations. Of the 100 largest budgets in the world, 49 are countries and 51 are corporations.[133] Drug deals move big money but drug dealing is not counted in the GDP, as it is illegal. Drug deals are illegal because illicit drug transactions are categorized as bad for people. But if they were counted everyone's goods and services would sky rocket. But those things are bad and we arrest bad people who do illegal things, at least such things as dealing drugs or prostitution because Capitalists are good. However damage to nature is bad. Evolution shows this clearly; from fossils to genes all life is related. Yet all this damage to nature is not illegal and is not counted as a minus to the GDP. Thus, we continue with this damage due to what current policy and marketing trends support. Obviously, this is not good.

THE CORPORATION AND TAXATION

Corporations have huge budgets, with many transactions, which are taxable—that is, if they are on paper. Corporations make a lot of money, which give them a lot of power. Corporations could easily solve the U.S. budget deficit—that is, if they paid taxes. An additional $250 billion of tax revenue would have been collected in 1996 if taxes had been collected at the same rate as they were from corporations in the 1950's.

Taxes have gone up for just about everyone I know, so it is rather slanted that the tax rate is something that has gotten smaller and smaller for billion dollar corporations. Not only do corporations receive huge tax breaks; the government gives them cash subsidies in the billions, $75 billion in 1998. The government also gives $60 billion to industry in specific tax breaks. And, that's not all, worldwide it is estimated that $235 billion to $350 billion is given in government subsidies for fossil fuel and nuclear energy facilities.[134] In other words, the government in this particular case directly subsidizes environmental genocide. How does this happen? Basically it is our addiction to oil allows this and soft money that continue it. When you add $75 billion to $60 billion it equals $135 billion,[135] which is a lot of solar panels and wind farms. The energy crisis could easily be solved by a shift to this type of renewable energy generation, with a fraction of the subsidies given to corporations and none of the pollution.

One Hollywood environmentalist, tired of poor, unpatriotic use of tax money, sent the IRS a note instead of full payment. Woody Harrelson told the IRS that he disagreed strongly with the government use of tax money to subsidize such industries as timber whose actions conflicted with the Endangered Species Act and Wilderness Act. He then informed them of where he donated his tax money, which was to aid the development of the domestic hemp industry. He ended his letter with this thought: "Two-hundred and twenty years ago we embarked on an historic journey to 'form a more perfect union' because we refused to submit to taxation without representation. Until my tax dollars stop going to subsidize destructive industries like timber, I cannot in good conscience continue to give...."[136] A final, very important note, when our country was founded the poor did not pay tax, only the rich, only those landholders with excessive income; the reverse now appears to be present.

DEALERS

Chemical, Oil, Gas, Timber, Pharmaceuticals, Financial Institutes, Agri-business, Retailers, Fashion, and even Universities all have the potential to be a type of dealer. If they fall in the arena where they push their product, convincing us that we cannot live without them or their product, whether we need the product or not they meet the definition of dealer. Dealers come in all shapes, sizes, economic avenues, colors, cultures, creeds, and dress. They all tend to be quite financially astute and have patterns that are recognizable with clear trails left in their wake. Toxic hot spots such as Penobscot River, Maine or the Lawrence River in New York, or the Fox River, Wisconsin and the Columbia River, Oregon are poisoned with dioxin and PCBs. These rivers run through the U.S. but toxic hot spots obviously exist across the globe. From San André, Brazil to Port Talbot United Kingdom to Tokyo, Japan to Quang Tri, Vietnam to Australia the world is inundated with a clear trail of toxins.

The way of the dealers is that of destruction. We live in a world where the dealers, both large and small take over the neighborhood, fill their pockets, watch the community crumble, then leave. Neighborhood after neighborhood, country after country, from Harlem, New York to the toxic dumps in the Philippines, they move in. From LA to

Korea they destroy with their chemicals of some form. From Miami to Timor there is violence that exceeds nightmare status. From London to Bangladesh they leave devastation for the poorest of poor to face. As for employees, they need to prove their worth, which varies with policy. Thus, there is a continual threat of losing their job due to non-compliance keeping a fear-based energy flowing.

Like Ray, the dealers count on sedation—sedation from fear, exhaustion, intimidation, ignorance, or apathy. They count on a pacified stance induced by the drug of choice. We hear about pollution. We hear about the latest downsizing. Recently CNN reported 6000 workers were let go at Coca-Cola Corporation in a major restructuring. In 1996 economists counted at least 500,000 jobs lost to free trade.[137] Last week it was another company downsizing. Last year they were relocating. Some move to Mexico, some to Korea, others to India looking for cheap labor and lax environmental laws. Since 1979 the Union of Workers has declined from 24% to 14%, even though 48% of workers say they would like a union.[138] We are losing jobs as labor rights become more vague. The New World Order isn't the friendliest place for everyone.

◆   ◆   ◆

Be it power or pleasure; corporations or consumers; or addicts or dealers there is a self-medicated stance to avoid a magnitude of dynamics. Like all addicts, we are our own worst enemy. We are vulnerable to the strategies of leaders whose beliefs are lost in the depths of power, money, and greed. Needless to say, the neighborhood has definitely gone down hill. Economics and a monetary based society ignite a most severe competition. Our safety lies in a failing comfort zone located between the new church and Starbucks. If we can look beyond our comfort zones and carefully constructed illusions it is easy to see that in the arena of this New World Order everything proves important in a most invisible way.

"When I first got here I thought you people were so wrong. I thought this place needed help.

It all seemed ridiculous. I thought I was right. The way I lived was right, and everyone else is wrong.

I was always so busy making my way right I didn't realize it was wrong."

—Anonymous

14

God the Product

"To be forgiven we first must believe in sin."

—Jewel

Sociologist William Martin stated concerning TV evangelists: "I thought (Swaggart) was one of the most honest, sincere preachers I had ever met. But I've seen him change over the years. He really seems to have been seduced by the power and the fame. I think what happens to this kind of person is that he begins to think, 'I couldn't have come this far if not for God.' Then he begins to say, 'Well, if I have this idea to build a Bible College or a mission it must come from God.' Next he starts to say, 'God told me this. God told me that…' And the next step from there is that he says, 'I think what God meant to say was…'[139]

At one time Oral Roberts said that God would call him home unless he raised $8.5 million. We probably should have let him go home under the pressure of these decisively high stakes. Then Swaggart followed with a sex scandal. And of course we cannot forget the Bakkers or the most recent dynamo of Jesse Jackson's fall from grace. Infidelity, embezzled funds, hidden children, foreign bank accounts, air conditioned dog houses, flash, dash and heavy make-up; no matter how bold the insanity, no matter how ridiculous the behavior, because these people had the audacity to perpetuate their wealth in the name of religiosity, in the name of God; money was sent in. The message resounds: 'Give to God. God understands the plan. He knows your sacrifices, plus we can build a new church with this money to impress Him.' Religion is man's way of impressing God. Somehow I don't think God is impressed.

WORSHIPPING THE GOD OF OPINION

Father Leo Booth says, "Religiously, politically, socially—as a species and as individuals—we have grown accustomed to someone else telling us what to do and when to do it, what is good for us and what isn't; what rewards await us when we obey (buy), and what punishments lie in store if we don't. Those doing the manipulating are always careful to let us think they have our best interests at heart and are equally careful to assure themselves that we won't dare question to question."[140]

People, out of generations of habit or a type of desperate need to believe in something, have bought into a belief system born by the use of religious oppression. Sometimes generations of imprints are like soul branding; tightly clamped vices on potentiality. God the product is an example of this very old tool where nothing is sacred. Religious addiction is used today just as it has been in the past. Religious addiction is using God, a church, or a belief system to escape reality in an attempt to feel better about our lives and our selves.[141]

Whoever prays the loudest and longest receives the nods and handshakes after church. Those sobbing trips to the altar are besieged with overjoyed parishioners full of support when one has been brought to one's knees and admits their sinful nature. How can we celebrate the collapse of an individual's mental state? How can we celebrate and validate a position of worthlessness? Religious addicts see themselves as worthless outside of their ability to serve God through the church.

Because of this worthless sense originating in their principal belief system, fed by manipulated religious teaching, religious addicts—active or not—never understand or get to experience true spirituality. They are functioning from a belief system they don't know the origins of. Be it blue collar Christians screaming and feuding amongst themselves or Country Club Christians with their apple-pie face and perfect image, they walk into church to be forgiven for patterns they will repeat. The rule of thumb here is if it looks good; it is good.[142] Like Ray, my million-dollar focused friends, and even Jack the god they're worshipping is once again the god of opinion.

RELIGIOUS ADDICTION

In *When God Becomes a Drug,* Father Leo Booth discusses a letter he received from a woman with religious addiction: "She wrote about her compulsive quoting of scriptural texts and her obsession with her own religious convictions, which led to arguments with family and co-workers. She described her eventual isolation from people she loved and her near bankruptcy caused by excessive tithing. She told me how she tried to escape feeling lonely, angry, depressed, fearful, and guilty by increasing her religious activities. The more she pursued her obsessive religiosity, the more helpless and isolated she became. She tried numerous times to stop her compulsive behavior by not going so frequently to church; removing statues, crucifixes, and incense burners from her home; not watching religious TV; hiding from members of her congregation; not returning telephone calls from her pastor and by canceling subscriptions for numerous religious magazines. Each time she relapsed into more severe religious addiction, causing greater guilt and shame. She finally sought counseling and eventually entered a treatment facility where she could undergo 'religious detox' in a safe environment."[143]

From the beginning of history, religion has acted as a drug. Eric Fromm clarifies religion as to "have a double function which is characteristic of every narcotic: They act as both an anodyne (painkiller) and as a deterrent too active change..." Father Booth sums religion up as having a three-fold function. "For all mankind religion is a consolation for the privations exacted by life. For the great majority of men, religion is encouragement to accept the class situation. And, for the dominant majority, religion is relief from guilt feelings caused by the suffering of those they oppress."

THE BEGINNING OF OPPRESSION AND CONTROL

George C. Williams in *The Pony Fish's Glow* discusses anthropologist Sarah Hardy's study of monkeys. Their mating system is a harem where dominant males have exclusive sexual access to a group of adult females as long as they can keep other males away. However, sooner or later a stronger male usurps the harem and the male he beats has to join the celibate outcasts. The new male power shows his love for the female by trying to kill their unweaned infants. For each successful killing a mother stops lactating and can be impregnated. Her baby's murderer fathers her next baby. William's asks: "Do you still think God is good?"[144]

There are always innocent bystanders. There are always changes in the landscape of life. The shift of power and its brutality is made obvious by research such as Sarah Hardy's. In different context, as spirituality not only became more secular but these sects were clarified into dominant religions; healthy skepticism became muted by threatening dogma, then a different form of violent dominance began its ascent.

During the early era of Christianity, there existed particular secular divisions that fed internal conflicts. Regardless of sect, if one was not of Roman decent, oppression was a part of life. Many Jews and Christians were extremely poor, some uneducated, and all deemed as 'less than' by the Romans. Romans taxed them heavily and denied them due process in regards to law; literally crucifying any overt expression that did not fall into the Roman's idea of normal. In this environment these early people of faith continuously rebelled against this abusive Roman rule.

In approximately 4BC one revolution appears to be a dominant catalyst towards control. In response to the secular uprising the Roman soldiers used warlike techniques to reinstate authority, killing thousands of civilians. Yet the movement against Roman rule continued, residing quietly, waiting for its moment with various new elements coming into play.

Around the time of Jesus' life, the Romans crucified 2000 revolutionary prisoners and again declared victory.[145] With the countryside riddled with crosses, which held the dead or dying the apocalyptic stories were born by the preaching of John the Baptist. This new sect, who are said to have included Jesus, are now commonly referred to as Christians; however, during these early centuries this sect also fed the already existing divisions that undermined any real attempt to overcome Roman rule; it gave the oppressed one more color; it provided the Romans with more internal conflict that fed their control.

The obvious separation between these oppressed lower classes and the more comfortable middle class grew and continued to bring increased conflict and violence. There evolved more secret sects and self-proclaimed visionaries who led guerrilla warfare on those who had more. Unrest was a sign of the times. One group of these 'Zealots' formed a secret sect called the 'Sacarii' who harassed, killed, and destroyed the peasant villages that would not join the revolt. This led to another full-blown revolt and eventual civil war, which again ended with Roman victory.

After this horrid civil war, resulting in the deaths of 100, 000 Jewish peasants and urban lower class a reemphasis on the apocalypse as the answer resurfaced. An end of the world theme seemed like a natural evolution when looking at the dominant energy and mentality of this time in history. Many embraced that only in death would they find life. And not only was this death imminent; no one would be left untouched by its hand. Judgment day seemed reasonable under the stress of their socio-economic prison. Their life surrounded an energy of hopelessness until religion entered the picture. The promise of eternal life in heaven gave them the will to go on. The glue that held them together was not only hope for a kinder eternal after-life, but a hatred of those of affluent lifestyle.[146]

For the next 250 years subtle oppression continued as did the expression 'natural economy.' Basically this was identified as the use of a hierarchical system with infinite dependencies. At the top there exists the emperor who everyone was supposed to love (but often secretly hated). And there were the aristocrats who everyone loved to hate, rightfully so, in those times their luxurious lives were far better than most.

In a very short period of time the Roman Empire became a rigid class structure that stagnated the poor and lower classes with this social system. It was regulated from the top, which in all appearances couldn't care less about the poor. The propaganda of religion began to take shape by way of the ruling class who saw other potential use for the dogma of the church. Thus this ruling class promptly postponed the apocalypse instigating an idealism that created an obedient lower class.

The bishops and the ruling class began to utilize religion's power with the poor to encourage them to behave. Not only was their socio-economic status stifled by the class system in obvious terms, religion's theme dictated certain conditions for entrance into heaven. This criteria included: renouncing the pleasures of the world, denying oneself, surrendering everything and anything to save their soul, and last but not least, have trust in God's grace through Jesus.

The wealthy saw these stipulations as absolutely appropriate. The stipulations were just one more pillow under the butt of aristocracy. As Eric Fromm so aptly states: "This was the fundamental transformation of Christianity from the religion of the oppressed to the religion of the rulers."[147] From the position of the poor, the prize was clear: they would get to heaven. And to further appease their need for some type of equalizing factor, those bad rich people would fall like rocks to the depth of Dante's hell—pillow or not, the Lord's wrath was infallible.

SHAME

As the wealthy and the government basked in their new found avenue of control over those they deemed 'weaker,' another element, shame, was added to control. Rabbi Heschel said, "Religion is the source of dissatisfaction with the self."[148] This dissatisfaction breeds on the propagation of shame, instigated by the church and religious dogma. The dark color of shame runs deep into the human psyche with ramifications that are still not fully understood. Augustine, a religious figure, authored a healthy contribution to shame's beginnings around 329BC.

Augustine's biographer, Peter Brown writes, "The story which Augustine tells in *The Confessions* is one of the most dramatic and massive evocations ever written of the evolution of the metaphysician; and his final 'conversion' to the idea of a purely spiritual reality, as held by sophisticated Christians in Milan, is a decisive and fateful step in the evolution of our ideas on spirit and matter."[149] Thus, as Mr. Brown identifies, Augustine was an enormous influence in current day definitive dogma; the power of his voice is undeniably a major part of the archetypes of our lives.

James Carroll continues clarifying Augustine's position "The point for Augustine was that whatever the aspects of the Godhead…are such to each other, they are in relation to each other. Relationship is the ground of divine being, an idea that opens up monotheism by moving meaning of God's oneness away from "unit" and toward "unity.""[150] Here Augustine seemed to have a positive role; he unified a very separatist mentality, which as we have seen undermined any organized strength for the oppressed and was the root of much of the secular conflict.

However, his tone shifts. There are many reasons for this as Augustine struggled with a multitude of issues—both emotional and political—that existed during his era. His writing reflected not only the secular Jewish-Christian conflict and an abusive Roman rule but also the energy initiated by the invasion of the Germanic's tribes. This invasion was a massive cultural trauma and added another dark color to the already near totalitarian regime. With or without conscious attempt, Augustine's writing and legacy reflects this violence declaring that the human condition implies a constant state, as James Carroll writes, of "finitude, weakness and sin."[151] The fall of man was clear; humans are born bad. This fall from grace was not only painful, but also blinding to we mere mortals. In the midst of the chaos of his life, it is hard to blame him for such a perception.

As a direct reflection of his perception, Augustine established what is known as the Trinitarian Doctorate, which set into motion the mass distribution of this shame-based theme with its punitive edge. Through his doctrine he then derived that the separation between God and man occurs and is maintained because of these circumstances of being born bad.

We still encounter his very black-white mentality in many churches to this day. And importantly, this type of shadow producing ideology feeds the martyr, feeds the shame, feeds the sense of worthlessness in a manner that is buried deep in the psyche of our archetypal memories, always showing up when looking at the motivation of any self-medication. There are few better reasons to self-medicate on a regular basis than the huge burden of being a victim of the original sin. The fall from grace leaves no stone unturned, no life form unattended, and a first-degree burn on our souls.

◆　　　◆　　　◆

Shame carries many nuances. Shame for an addict is tough because when you address all that has gone wrong and all the problems the addiction has caused, the addict doesn't feel guilt for screwing up; they feel shame because these consequences prove to them that they *are* bad. The "I am bad" archetypal belief is fed. With this premise in place all advice feels like a personal attack, creating a defensive, guarded stance. This shame short-circuits the whole system of how feelings are processed creating a lack of self-esteem, self-respect, and self-confidence. This shame also undermines any self-discipline, self-control or self-determination. And primarily it incapacitates self-love,[152] which is the door to self-actualization and facilitates the dynamics of all relationships including family interactions, inheritance, and ultimately World Peace, Emotional Prosperity, Environmental Sanctity, and Eternal Serenity.

THE ETERNALLY WOUNDED

Our entrapment is often conceived in generations of beliefs, imprints, fear-based energy, and an ill collective conscious, which are fed by pseudo-religions who manipulate and distort core biblical teachings. Many of the gospel parables are reiterated to shame people utilizing a punitive edge. In a pyramid structure of government it is best to make the ultimate power one that is vengeful.

From early Romans to France to England to Western civilization a shame-based sense of self has been and is fed by religion. From Constantine to St. James everyone put their power-based two-cents into the melting pot of religious dogma. When leaders during the Renaissance moved to mass-produce the Bible, religion was again seen as a way to control the masses. Bible stories were edited many times over the centuries[153] and if the editor was consumed with power they would distort the story as to utilize the control it offered. However they saw life, however disturbed their vision was, it still gets relayed by this age-old source that few question.

"Go to church or you'll go to hell," is a powerful image and it does get the masses through the doors for a weekly dose of shame. People who are scared and feel bad about themselves don't tend to rebel. They don't make waves or question the ruling class. They feel too bad about themselves and with their self-esteem in the dumpster they have little motivation to confront bias and distorted doctrine. Eventually many could not escape their unhappiness; despair still lingering even within the walls of the ornate. Relief from emptiness was sought. Commercialism then found its niche.

Disturbed dogma that attempts to influence a society with the use of shame gives way for an over burgeoning ego. "Our souls are tossed to the earth," as Mary Ann Williamson says, "and we are scorched by such a low descent." Scarred and confused, somehow we need to find out that there is more to life than accepting our shameful origins. Conditioned to seek out the entrance card to our salvation, being impatient as we are, we do drugs, shop, eat, drink, or we just want more and more and more. At some point we realize that there is a gigantic gap between 'doing good' and 'being good.' Then we learn the difference between acting peaceful and being peaceful.

Our wounds are deep. We search for a power, often referred to as God, who we are taught very young is a jealous, vengeful entity that will send us to hell should we displease him. This Christian God who is magnified in the Western World seems to make more victims than saviors, a sort of Alice in Wonderland with sore knees, an easy to read version of scripture, constant cravings, closet phobias, and chest pains.

Whether we remember it or not, we're resigned to the archetype that the 'hand of God' is a 'mean one' like the Grinch. Regardless of excessive inconsistencies, errors in judgment, and inaccuracies that constantly trip us up, the search continues—sometimes drunk, sometimes sober.

◆   ◆   ◆

Though religion is full of horrid actions in the name of God, I am not so sure the Creator of the universe would agree to its tyranny. Creation is of a different energy. Ultimately, the most potent deceit of all is looking for our holiness outside of ourselves.

"There's an old saying in AA that states: 'I drink the poison expecting you to die.'
Makes sense doesn't it?"

—Fred, 22 years sober

PART V
A Matter of One

o o o o o o o o o o o o o o o o o o o o o o o o o o o o o o o o o

"Schopenhauer…

Points out that when you reach an advanced age and look back over your lifetime, it can seem to have had a consistent order and plan, as though composed by some novelist.

Events that when they occurred had seemed accidental and of little moment turn out to have been indispensable factors in the composition of a consistent plot.

So who composed the plot?

Schopenhauer suggests that just as your dreams are composed by an aspect of yourself of which your conscious is unaware, so, too, your whole life is composed by the will within you.

And just as people whom you will have met apparently by mere chance became leading agents in the structuring of your life, so too, will you have served unknowingly as an agent, giving meaning to the lives of others.

The whole thing gears together like one big symphony with everything unconsciously structuring everything else…one great dream of a single dreamer in which all the dream characters dream, too."

—*Turbulent Mirror, An Illustrated Guide to Chaos Theory and the Science of Wholeness*
John Briggs & F. David Peat

15

Creation and Coincidences

"Nothing is more powerful than an individual acting out of their conscious, thus helping bring the collective conscious to life."

—Norman Cousins

In the movie Sphere, the characters figure out that they have been given a gift, that their thoughts create their reality almost instantaneous. With this creation there arrives monsters, paranoia, and destruction. It takes a while for the characters to figure out what is going on, but once they get it their perception of the problem is altered. They begin to act from a place of communal wellness versus fear. After being blatantly shown not only the power of their thoughts, but the fact that their thoughts go the direction of harmful creations they realize the degree of responsibility they have. In the end they 'will' this gift away and recognize their inability to handle such power.

BEYOND CREATION

There is this Far Side cartoon on one of my son's calendars. It has this guy standing outside of a building with two doors. One door says 'Damned if you do' while the other door says 'Damned if you don't.' Then behind this poor sap is the devil, poking him in the butt with his pitchfork to make a decision. Change feels like a huge step into a terrifying horizon of the unknown with all the soul searching and confession that addicts have passionately avoided. In all addiction the first step towards sanity is admitting that there is a problem. Learning that our disagreements do not dismantle the past; they build a wider future.

Our ability to choose our lives is an enormous gift. We can choose to not be victims and if you take nothing else from this book I hope you remember the power of your thoughts, words, and deeds. Each of us is a powerful co-creator of this world. We have the genetics of people who worked their way from indentured servitude and slaves to renters to stockholders. We transformed ourselves into successful men and women. And ultimately, we find we are successful Americans who can afford amazing habits. (By the way it was always the rich addicts that ended up killing themselves, the poor ones couldn't afford enough of their drug to get there.)

So if we can afford to kill ourselves we surely can afford the sweat it will take to save ourselves. This nation was built on our ancestor's tears, blood, and sweat. This nation continues on ours. Though much in history focuses on the writers of the Declaration of Independence and its authors, there were many heroes. Our forefathers, with their obvious faults and conflicting data, did plant the seed that has grown into the degree of freedom we enjoy.

Whether we were born from religious freedom or greed or basic rebellion we are now in a position of knowledge and ability to perpetuate freedom. Our wellness is at risk as we misplace our energies. Nature reflects this decline. Coincidences give us hint after hint. Until we redefine our priorities and confront our illnesses we will continue to watch all that has been built crumble.

ATTENTION

Where there is life there is always a search for something—be it meaning, money, or supper. Ralph Waldo Emerson says: "Where do we find ourselves? In a series of which we do not know the extremes, and believe that it has none. We wake and find ourselves on a stair; there are stairs below us, which we seem to have ascended; there are stairs

above us, many a one, which go upward and out of sight."[154] One
extreme after another holds our attention hostage. Be it this incident or
that problem, life is riddled with an imbalance of experience, which
introduce moments of balance—sometimes looking down from a roof,
up from an ER gurney, or simply when the money runs out for the
'more' that is suffocating.

Attention eventually breaks free; the bogeyman gets spooked, trips
over the toys, and we see beyond the mundane. Greg Levoy says in
Callings: "No amount of intellectual authority, arrogant confidence,
name dropping, or ego and ambition pounding on the door demanding to be admitted will allow us passage. Beyond a certain point, faith
is the magic lamp and humility is the abracadabra."[155] Consciously
realigning our attention is basic as we jump headfirst into what feels to
be an illogical ocean of faith. Thus it is indeed this leap of faith where
hope is found and where new heights of buried humility are introduced.

When the barrage of data that has held our attention disintegrates
into the meaningless space from which it came, we are freed. This is
that step beyond intellect where faith begins and where we find the
divine. We feel the sacred nature of life. It is, without question, a space
that is preserved by faith and a place that only can exist in the empire
of our attention. Should we get lost in details or desires, again, cravings
will take hold. As Marianne Williamson says, we are too quick to give
up our daily reading, meditation or whatever it is that keeps us sane.

SOBRIETY

The crux of sobriety is staying awake and taking precautions so one
doesn't get sucked back into the cycle of use. Being part of life, being
part of creation involves this road to wakefulness. It has nothing to do
with our car drive, education, employment status, or the square footage
of our house. It is not associated with a certain religion or civic stance.
It has to do with inner awareness and serenity. This wakeful position is

different for everyone. I always thought that we are here to 'get it.' And I don't mean sex or shot or revenge or the winning lottery ticket. We're here to understand what we need to understand as souls.

For everyone it is different. For the murderer, it's not to kill. For the Narcissist, it's to see others as important. For the thief, it's not to steal. For the addict it's not to use something to medicate feelings. For the corporate CEO it is possibly compassion. For the control freak it's letting go. For the logger it is to appreciate the forest for more than its timber. For the perfectionist it's acceptance of all levels of creation.

We are here to learn and experience. All learning curves are different. All paths are different. From genetic resentment to facing our own personal hell, to ghosts real or imagined, we are here to experience these dynamics. This is why all competitiveness is absurd. We seem to have gotten stuck in oral fixations, anxiety, aggression, and money mentality trying to satisfy the inner self; we got stuck trying to win a game that doesn't exist. There is no right or wrong, good or bad, or even sinner or saint. There is only the act of becoming.

The process is the key; one of re-socialization, restructuring needs verses wants, questioning beliefs and behaviors, and connection; the process of listening to all that is around us. Life is more than a series of events. Life is full a little flash cards that guide us to where we need to be. These flash cards are pieces to the puzzle of life. Some see them as coincidences, I see them as divine guidance because as you pay attention to them they become not only clearer but occur more often. Maybe it is simply the act of paying attention that seems to bring clarity, where our attention falls is a powerful thing.

As we behave differently, we feel different and are less prone to addiction's ploys. But we must stay still long enough to engage in a process. We must stay long enough to face our dragons with acceptance and forgiveness verses death by the sword. As we follow the coincidences of life we are able to see how our energy affects those around us. When we are kind, others are kind. When we believe in our abundance and the abundance of the universe, we always have enough. We also can see when we are rude how those around us are less than hospitable and we can see that there are times that no matter how kind we are, the energy we are confronting will stay in a negative realm. We learn that this is okay.

Our expectations damper the divine, taking the joy out of our interactions and turning life into pressure. Expectations place a strangle hold on acceptance. This is important because it is in acceptance that we find serenity. Serenity is a process that is continually being created with the new positioning of our lives. As long as we seek serenity we will see it surface, the situations in our lives will feed it and at times challenge it. The challenge allows us to compare where we are, where we have been, and where we can go.

The eternal process of creation happens in each moment with the energy we bring to the moment. Healing the world involves peaceful moments and peaceful actions. Healing our world involves connecting which in turn means talking and listening. When we find out something is hurtful or helpful, we spread the news. Boycotts are simple; you just don't buy a certain product. There are a lot of deviant corporations that thrive on the fact that many do not boycott their products even when their slave labor techniques are brought to light. A key to remember is that when slave labor is in one place it has the potential, like a fungus, to spread to other places. Look at what has happened to the living wage in America, what has happen to labor jobs, and the reduction in many factory-based salaries. Thus being awake and attentive is vital, then following through is even more critical. Being awake is simple; read more, listen more, share more, look around more, and watch TV a lot less. Or, get rid of it totally. You'd be amazed at how different life is. How much color is added to reality.

TREATMENT

Shifting one's life to no longer entertain addiction needs to be holistic, focusing on the damaging quality of various belief systems, self-concepts, and behaviors integrating socially conscientious data. Account-ability and responsibility are not only the beginning but also a part of the process.

As we begin the process of self-actualization it effects those near and far. When getting in touch with feelings it reconnects us to our inner self; thus we are reconnected to all that exists. The core of any thera-peutic treatment is this search for feelings. We as therapists do many things to help addicts get in touch with their feelings. We go to great lengths and utilize an array of approaches. It is surprising what event happens to turn on a light, bring down a wall, or flood a heart with warmth.

When I worked in treatment centers we had our addicts write a lot of letters. Letters to fathers, mothers, sisters, brothers, dead people, and to themselves. We did field trips to Glenn Helen. We did the obstacle course whenever possible. We held groups in parking lots, on hospital roofs, playgrounds, cafeterias, and hospital rooms. We even held a group on the sidewalk outside my then young son's elementary school, so bullies would see this dozen or so rough looking cartel pick up my son with me. My son was never bullied again and the addicts went from bad guys to heroes instantly, even though three police cars (all the police of that little town) showed up and watched our little procession.

Needless to say we got in trouble for some of it as unethical or not proven. But we continued. We set free balloons with resentments, thank you notes, hopes, dreams, and sometimes-even feelings. We did walks, runs, work programs, and art projects. We did a lot of collages. There was a lot of listening, a lot of silence and brutal honesty. But addicts got better and we counselors did too. The administration rarely did get better though; they generally stayed on the wrong page because their wellness never left the halls of budget and profit margins.

PLAN A

Feelings, whatever their nature, are a good place to start when looking at change. Feelings are such amazing motivation. We feel strongly about our children and our family. They hold many doors and many keys. My children hold much power with me. They woke me up. I didn't want children but the cosmic powers that be had other plans. I have three. All conceived or delivered outside of wedlock, which still makes my mother reel. My sixteen-year-old Adam was born on Thanksgiving, right after the wedding. My nine-year-old Jesse was born on Mother's Day, right after the divorce and my little girl Olivia, eight, was born the next Father's Day, a product of a brief, unsuccessful reconciliation.

So it has been these three children and me. I think they were sent on holidays so I would get the divine order process that has become the dominant theme of my life. Parenting is tough and I am not good at it. I have no idea what I am doing. But we get through moment by moment and seem to evolve, which is the way of learning. In these many moments they have taught me about patterns, life, and what's important. When I look at them I couldn't imagine the pain if I had to watch them go hungry, had no bed to tuck them into with soft blankets, or watch one go fight in a feudal war with the potential of not returning.

When I see the billions of people in dire circumstances, my heart goes out to them. Their children are my children. The older people are my parents. When I make them real I feel and when I feel I want to live differently. As I internalize their reality as my own, I touch on the actuality of their life. I connect to the bigger picture. They are our brothers and sisters. Everything is connected.

RECOVERY

Recovery is a process of mending; thus, help always arrives as avenues materialize. When we believe that good can win, it will win. Our children win. Creation wins. Changing the world happens one by one. Be it a feeling or divinity or the love for a child, feelings are energy; and all energy is connected. When we connect to an energy greater than ourselves we no longer struggle for power or energy because we are connected to the source. All recovery is different with different roles and paths.

Some paths initiate legislation and some paths are about bravery; the ability to challenge current day thinking by taking a stand, being part of a protest or by living differently. Some may write a lot of letters. I write a lot of letters: letters to Senators, Congressmen, Mayors, Legislators, the President, or Editors. Perhaps you will write letters to dead people or yourself like some of the clients needed to. Or maybe you will put a wind turbine on your house to generate your own energy freeing yourself from the grips of the utility industry and its many polluting ways. Maybe you will put a cistern system on your property to recycle water, grow your own food showing Agri-business you won't tolerate their poisonous ways, go vegan, turning your back on eating animal products altogether, get an electric car, or use biodiesel and drive around smelling like French fries or donuts versus Carbon Monoxide.

You can do field trips to Washington to advocate sound policy, to the Ancient Forests to protect them from the timber industry's chain saws, to India to help the sick, or next door to finally get to know your neighbor. If you stumble onto an obstacle course, go for it whenever possible. Have meetings in parking lots, on hospital roofs, playgrounds, cafeterias, hospital rooms, or wherever you need to. Get in trouble for some of it; it is okay.

Remember, image is meaningless, the god of opinion is dead; there is no one left to impress. The main thing is to continue. To clearly look at beliefs and behaviors, to question, doubt, then put into motion the change needed to live harmlessly. Turn off the TV. Put the novel down and read some books about what is really going on in the environment and the world. Do a lot of listening, a lot of silence and a lot of brutal honesty. The biggest shift is of the soul. We are seeing the power of our individual creativeness. There are many ways we are seeing this shift materialize. And one is the acceptance of our connected position. Nature is teaching us that if we destroy one part of her, the rest will be harmed—nature's health and life depends on its connectedness. Our health depends on our connectedness. The search for the divine is no less a search for survival.

◆   ◆   ◆

The reality that we are the collective conscious is materializing with more clarity daily. The world's future, our future, our children's future depends on us as individuals. Thoughts evolve into reality continuously. It is time for us to think for ourselves again. It is time to stop giving our power away for a cheap, insincere compliment or a day in the mall.

We are at the edge of something huge, teetering between a total rejuvenation of much, much kinder times or total despair. Walking the edge together or individually equates an energy to existence that blows status quo out of the water and breathes life into day to day drudgery. It is on this edge we awaken and remember we are a part of something very noble. The enormity of our position will not fade into the shadows: the time has arrived for us to embrace the challenge and undertake our true reason for being here. We will create a new dance. We will emerge a kinder culture. We might even save the world.

In uncharted territory is where life begins. Within these new territories are not genetically altered food but small community gardens, conservation, a respect for all life, and a lot of historic American ingenuity. We find peace in physically connecting to those who we are already eternally connected with. We will choose not to pull the trigger or scream or plan revenge or whatever our trepidation is—instead we will choose to understand. No matter how much the ego shouts to punish, defile, or to bring righteous justice we remain dedicated to a divine plan that is in the making, trusting in something greater than ourselves; something that somehow has taken on a life of its own within us. It is staying in the fields of openness and forgiveness that gives us strength.

Our wellness is derived from internal peace verses a financial number placed before us by a society that has shown there is simply never enough. Recovery from addiction is recovery from many beliefs, realities, traditions, habits, scripts, archetypes, behaviors, things, ways, and from the rigors of 21st century life itself. It is, without question, no easy task.

We are all still basically renters. We borrow the land from our children, as they will borrow it from theirs. For it is the process of life that continues to seek itself again and again. And we are the powerful agents that affect the process. My goal in writing this book was to get you thinking and feeling again. So if you are angry, good, at least you are feeling and connecting. I have touched a nerve. Something you already knew at some level. What you do with it is up to you. Recovery and individual paths are so different. From this point on the journey is yours. And whatever playgrounds you decide upon I wish you well.

"She followed her lover everywhere—into parking lots with strangers, into dark cars, into the shadows along steep mountain roads, into apartments that smelled like stale smoke and had three or four locks on every door. When her lover wasn't with her, she

was left with her own terror of how to move through the world alone."

—Patti Davis, Dope: A Love Story, Time May 7,2001

Epilogue: A Last Resort

"The wind, one brilliant day, called."

—Antonio Machado

The tree sitters in California trying to save the Ancient forests are some of the bravest people of the new millennia. As Julia Butterfly Hill states: "Tree-sitting is a last resort. When you see someone in a tree trying to protect it, you know that every level of our society has failed. The consumers have failed, the companies have failed, and the government has failed. Friends of the forests have gone to courts, activists have tried to make consumers aware, but with no results. Corporations have neglected their responsibility as landowners, while government has refused to enforce its laws. Everything has failed, so people go into the trees."

Killing a forest is killing our self. Aside from the obvious atrocity and the total disrespect for life that is revealed we kill a part of our being. Again, everything is eternally connected. The energy of any natural system gives answers that are overwhelming clear and hold the essence of life everywhere. Some of those who understand this go sit in trees. They are challenging current day issues with this one peaceful act. So if you still feel lost and want some form of direction at this point: go sit in a tree...the answers will come.

"I followed the white lines of coke on mirror after mirror.
In the end there was only the mirror left. I had to look at myself."

—Patti Davis, Dope: A Love Story, Time May 7,2001

Endnotes

1. Sobel, David, *Galileo's Daughter*, (Penguin Books 2000), pg. 153

2. Cooper, William, *Behold a Pale Horse*, (Light Technology Publishing, 1991) pg 40-41

3. "A Dose of Reality," *Adbusters* Jul/Aug 2001, pg. 16

4. Montague, Peter, PhD., "One Fundamental Problem,"*Rachel's Environment and Health Weekly* #582, 1/22/98. pg. 2. [online] URL: **http://www.rachel.org**.

5. Montague, Peter, PhD., "New Strategy Focus on Corporations," *Rachel's Environment and Health Weekly* #309, 1995, pg. 2. [online] URL: **http://www.rachel.org**

6. Quindlen, Anna, "Honestly-You Shouldn't Have," *Newsweek*, December 3, 2001, pg 76.

7. Schlosser, Eric, *Fast Food Nation*, (Houghton Mifflin, 2001) pg. 4

8. Lasn, Kalle, *Culture Jam, The Uncooling of America*, (Eagle Book, 1999), pg. 9

9. Hartmann, Thom, *The Last Hours of Ancient Sunlight*, (Mythical Books, 1996) pp. 76-80

10. Hartmann, pp. 76-80

11. Hartmann, pp. 42-43

12. "Monsanto," pg.8, WEB: **http://users.netropolis.net/timjim/monsanto.htm**.

13. Ridgeway, James & St. Clair, Jeffrey, *A Pocket Guide To Environmental Bad Guys (and a few ideas on how to stop them)*, (Thunder Mouth Press, 1998) pg. 114, pp.178.

14. Brink, Susan, "Your Brain On Alcohol," *Newsweek* May 7,2001, pgs. 50-57

15. Carroll, James, *Constantine's Sword, The Church and the Jews: A History*, (Houghtlin Mifflin Company, 2001)

16. Close, Frank, *Lucifer's Legacy, The Meaning of Asymmetry*, (Oxford, 2000), pg. 1

17. Huffington, Arianna, *How to Overthrow the Government*, (Regan Books, Harper Collins 2000) pg. xvii

18. Huffington, pg. xvii

19. Huffington, pg. xvii

20. Needleman, Jacob, *Money and the Meaning of Life*, (Currency and Doubleday, 1991), pg. 66

21. Needleman, pg. 77

22. Mander, Jerry, Goldsmith, Edward, *The Case Against the Global Economy and For A Turn Toward the Local*, (Sierra Club Books, 1996), pg. 109

23. **http://www.ewg.org** (The Environmental Working Group conducted the survey of the Freedom to Farm Act).

24. Schlosser, pg 37

25. Schlosser, Eric, *Fast Food Nation*, (Houghton Mifflin, 2001) pp. 40-41

26. Schlosser, pg 43

27. Schlosser, pg 46

28. Rasmussen, V., "Rethinking the Corporation," *Food and Water Journal*, Fall 1998. pg. 19

29. Rasmussen, pg. 19

30. Galbraith, John, K., *The Affluent Society*, (New American Library, 1984), pg. 121

31. Galbraith, pg. 1

32. Renner, Michael, *Fighting for Survival*, (W.W. Norten, 1996), pg. 81

33. CNN, November 29,1999

34. Ridgeway, James & St. Clair, Jeffrey, *A Pocket Guide To Environmental Bad Guys (and a few ideas on how to stop them)*, (Thunder Mouth Press, 1998) pg. 94-95, pp. 178

35. Montague, Ph.D., P., "Landfills are Dangerous, September 24, 1998", *Rachel's Environment & Health Weekly*, #617, pg. 2 Attributed to: Budnick, L. D., and others, "Cancer and birth defects near the Drake Superfund Site, Pennsylvania," *Archives of Environmental Health*, Vol. 39, No. 6 (November 1984) pgs. 409-413

36. Montague, pg. 2

37. Montague, pg. 2

38. Montague, pg. 2

39. Clapp, R. W., Cobb S., Chan, C.K., and Walker Jr., B. "Leukemia (sic)Near Mass Power Plant," *The Lancet*, Dec. 5 1987, pgs. 1324-1325

40. Montague, Ph.D., P., "Landfills are Dangerous, September 24, 1998," *Rachel's Environment & Health Weekly*, #617, pg. 2

41. Montague, pg. 2

42. Sanjour, Wm.,"What's Wrong with the EPA, August 20, 1998,"*Rachel's Environment & Health Weekly*, #612, pg. 1

43. Giuliano, Ph.D., Jackie Alan, "Earth Day 2000-To March or To Shop?" *Healing Our World: Weekly Comment, Environmental*

News Service, April 24, 2000, pg. 3 WEB: **http:// ens.lycos.com/ens/apr2000/2000L-04-19g.html**

44. Gore, Al, *Earth in the Balance*, (Plume: Penguin,) pg. 151

45. Giuliano, Ph.D., Jackie, Alan, "Its Official—Greed is Killing Us," *Healing Our World: Weekly Comment*, May 1999 pg. 1, WEB: **http://www.ens.lycos.com/ens/may99/1999L-05-09g.html**

46. "Breath-taking: Premature Mortality Due to Particulate Air Pollution in 29 American Cities," a May 1996 report by the Natural resources Defense Council. WEB: **http://www.org/find/ aibresum.html**

47. Giuliano, Ph.D., Jackie, Alan, "Its Official—Greed is Killing Us," *Healing Our World: Weekly Comment*, May 1999 pg. 1 WEB: **http://www.ens.lycos.com/ens/may99/1999L-05-09g.html**

48. Lazaroff, Cat, "Benefits of Clean Air Regs Top Costs by a Margin of Four to One," *Environmental News Network*, November 17, 1999, pg 1. WEB: **http://ens.lycos.com/ens/nov99/ 1999L-11-17-07.html**.

49. Renner, Michael, *Fighting for Survival*, (W.W. Norten, 1996), pg. 81

50. WEB: **http://www.who.int/**

51. "By the Numbers," *Time, Special Edition, Spring 2000, pg. 90*

52. Ryan, John, C., Durning, Alan, Thein, *Stuff The Secret Lives of Everyday Things*, (Northwest Environment Watch 1997) pg. 55

53. Lazaroff, Cat, "Growing population Faces Diminishing Resources," *Environmental News Service*, January 18,2000, pg. 2. WEB: **http://ens.lycos.com/ens/jan2000/2000L-01-18-06.html**.

54. Brown, Lester, R., Flavin, Christopher, French, Hilary, et.al., *State of the World 2000*, (The Worldwide Institute, 2000), pp. 42-50

55. Brown, pp. 42-50

56. Giuliano, Ph.D., Jackie, Alan, "Its Official—Greed is Killing Us," *Healing Our World: Weekly Comment*, May 1999 pg. 2 WEB: **http://www.ens.lycos.com/ens/may99/1999L-05-09g.html**

57. Hartmann, T., *The Prophets Way*, (Mystical Books, 1995) pg. 97-99.

58. Montague, P., "Pesticides and Children: A Case Study," *Food and Water Journal, Summer, 1999* pg. 35

59. Montague, P.,"Drinking Water and Leukemia, June 6, 1988," *Rachel's Environment & Health Weekly*, #80, pg. 2

60. "How Your Tax Dollars Help Bring Polluters Into Your Neighborhood," *Sierra Club*, pg. 1 of 5, **http://www.sierraclub.org/cafos/report99/intro.asp**.

61. Montague, P. Ph.D., "The Regulatory-Industrial Complex," *Rachel's Environment & Health Weekly*, #238, pg. 2

62. Wm. Sanjour, "What's Wrong With The EPA," *Rachel's Environment & Health Weekly*, #612, August 20, 1998, pg. 1

63. Montague, Ph.D., P., "New Strategy Focuses On Corporations," *Rachel's Environment & Health Weekly*, #309, October 28, 1992, pg.1

64. Monotague, Ph.D., P., "One Fundamental Problem," *Rachel's Environment & Health Weekly*, #582, pg. 4. Attributed data to: Classen, D.C., and others, "Adverse Drug Events in Hospitalized Patients", *Journal of the American Medical Association (JAMA)* Vol. 277, No. 4 (January 22/29 1997), pgs. 301-306

65. "The Planet—Right to Sue, The Hidden War on the Environment", *The Sierra Club,* pg. 1of 2, **http://www.sierraclub.org/planet/199502/war1.html**

66. Robbins, John, *Diet for a New America,* (HJ Kramer 1987) pg. 250

67. Levoy, Gregg, *Callings, Finding and Following an Authentic Life,* (Three Rivers Press, paperback ed. 1998), pg. 10

68. Kotulak, Ronald, *Inside the Brain Revolutionary Discoveries of How The Mind Works,* (Andrews McMeel Publishing, 1996), pp. 116-119

69. Kotulak, pp. 38

70. Kotulak, pp. 78-83

71. Kotulak, pp. 69

72. Roger D. Masters, Brian Hone, and Anil Doshi, "Environmental Pollution, Neurotoxicity, and Criminal Violence," in J. Rose, editor, ENVIRONMENTAL TOXICOLOGY (In press. London and New York: Gordon and Breach Publishers, 1997)

73. Motluck, Allison,"Pollution may lead to a life of crime," NEW SCIENTIST Vol 154, No. 2084 (May 31, 1997), pg. 4

74. C.E. Koop and G.D. Lundberg, "Violence in America: A Public Health Emergency," JOURNAL OF THE AMERICAN MEDICAL ASSOCIATION," Vol. 267, No. 22 (1992), pgs. 3075-3076

75. O'Reilly, Bill, *The O'Reilly Factor,* (Broadway, 2000), pg. 39

76. Pratkanis, Anthony, Aronson, Elliot, *Age of Propaganda, The Everyday Use and Abuse of Persuasion,* (Freeman Press, 1991), pg. 50

77. Pratkanis, pg. 4-5

78. Brown, Lester, R., Flavin, Christopher, French, Hilary, et.al., *State of the World 2000*, (The Worldwide Institute, 2000), pg. 74

79. Brown, pg. 76

80. Brown, pg. 68

81. Pratkanis, Anthony, Aronson, Elliot, *Age of Propaganda, The Everyday Use and Abuse of Persuasion*, (Freeman Press, 1991), pg. 50

82. Mander, Jerry, *Four Arguments For The Elimination of Television*, (Quill, 1978), pg. 225

83. Hartmann, T., *The Prophets Way*, (Mystical Books, 1995) pgs. 97-99.

84. Postman, Neil, *Amusing Ourselves to Death, Public Discourse in the Age of Show Business*, (Penguin, 1985), pg. 3

85. Postman, pg. 3

86. Postman, pg. 6

87. Pratkanis, Anthony, Aronson, Elliot, *Age of Propaganda, The Everyday Use and Abuse of Persuasion*, (Freeman Press, 1991), pg. 11

88. Crossen, Cynthia, *Tainted Truth: The Manipulation of Fact in America*, (Simon & Schuster 1996), pg. 19

89. Crossen, pg. 19

90. Crossen, Cynthia, *Tainted Truth: The Manipulation of Fact in America*, (Simon & Schuster, 1996), pg. 12-13

91. Crossen, pg. 19

92. Flint, R. W., PhD, Houser, W.L. MRC, *Living a Sustainable Lifestyle: forOur Children's Children*, (Writers Club Press 2001)

93. Greer, Jed & Bruno, Kenny, *Greenwash The Reality Behind Corporate Environmentalism,* (Third World Network and The Apex Press, 1996), pg.11

94. Greer, pg. 59

95. Saul, John Ralston, *The Unconscious Civilization,* (Free Press, 1997), pg. 91

96. Saul, pg. 18-19

97. Levoy, Gregg, *Callings, Finding and Following and Authentic Life,* (Three Rivers Press, paperback ed. 1998), pg. 43

98. Dilts, Robert, *Beliefs Pathways to Health and Well-Being,* (Metamorphous Press, 1990), pg. 30

99. Dilts, pg. 47

100. Dilts, pgs. 29-60

101. Caroll, James, *Constantine's Sword The Church and the Jews: A History* (Houghtlin Mifflin Company, 2001), pg. 179

102. Chomsky, Noam, *Media Control the Spectacular Achievements of Propaganda,* (Seven Stories Press/New York 1997), pp. 5-17

103. Kellman, Peter, "Freedom of Association, Final Part" *Rachel's Environment and Health Weekly* # 701, June 15, 2000, pg. 2

104. Chomsky, Noam, *Media Control the Spectacular Achievements of Propaganda,* (Seven Stories Press/New York, 1997), pp. 5-17

105. Chomsky, pp. 10 & 17

106. Berman, Morris, *The Twilight of American Culture,* (W.W. Norton & Company, 2000), pp. 33-39

107. Dilts, Robert, *Beliefs Pathways to Health and Well-Being,* (Metamorphous Press, 1990), pp. 1-50

108. Pratkanis, Anthony, Aronson, Elliot, *Age of Propaganda, The Everyday Use and Abuse of Persuasion*, (Freeman Press, 1991), pg. 36

109. Pratkanis, pp. 33-35

110. Hartmann, T., *The Prophets Way*, (Mystical Books, 1995), pp. 97-99

111. Matthay, Camy, "Unschooling as a Political Activity," *Food and Water Journal*, Fall 2000, pp. 16-23

112. Loewen, James, W., *The Lies My Teacher Told Me*, (Simon & Schuster, 1996), pg. 148

113. Kellman, Peter, "Labor Organizing and Freedom of Association," *Rachel's Environment and Health Weekly* # 697, May 18,2000. Sited: Levine, Bruce, & et. al., *Who Built America*, Vol. 1 (Pantehon Books, 1989), pg 25

114. Kellman, pg. 25

115. Kellman, pg. 25

116. Kellman, pg. 26

117. Loewen, James, W., *The Lies My Teacher Told Me*, (Simon & Schuster, 1996) pp. 146-148

118. Kellman, Peter, "Labor Organiazing and Freedom of Association," *Rachel's Environment and Health Weekly* # 697, May 18,2000. Sited: Fresia, Jerry, Toward An American Revolution, (Boston South End Press, 1988), pg. 26

119. Korten, David C., *The Post Corporate World*,(Berrett-Koehler Publishers, Inc., and Kumerian Press,Inc., 1999), pg. 76

120. Korten, pg. 59

121. Korten, pg. 59

122. Huffington, Arianna, *How to Overthrow the Government*, (Regan Books, Harper Collins, 2000), pg. 2

123. Rasmussen, V., "Rethinking the Corporation,"*Food &Water Journal*, Fall 1998, pg. 19

124. Needleman, Jacob, *Money and the Meaning of Life*, Currency and Doubleday, 1991, pg. 33

125. "A Survey of Multinationals," *Economist*, Mar.27, 1993, pp. 5-6

126. Korten, David C., *When Corporations Rule the World*, (Kumerian Press, 1995, 1996), pg. 83

127. Korten, pg. 110

128. Korten, pg. 130

129. Korten, pg. 129

130. Nader, Ralph, et. al., *The Case Against Free Trade*, (Earth Island Press 1993), pg. 7

131. Galbraith, John, K., *The Affluent Society*, New American Library, 1984, pg. 48

132. Korten, David C., *The Post Corporate World*, (Berrett-Koehler Publishers, Inc., and Kumerian Press,Inc., 1999), pg. 70 & Chapter 3

133. Loewen, James, W., *The Lies My Teacher Told Me*, (Simon & Schuster 1996) pp. 38-73

134. Korten, David C., The Post *Corporate World*, (Berrett-Koehler Publishers, Inc., and Kumerian Press,Inc., 1999), pp. 47-48

135. Korten, pp. 47-48

136. Werbach, Adam, *Act Now, Apologize Later*, (Sierra Club, 1997) pp. 77-81

137. Dawkins, Kristin, *Gene Wars: The Politics of Biotechnology*, (Seven Stories Press, 1997) pg. 11

138. Kellman, Peter, "Labor Organiazing and Freedom of Association," *Rachel's Environment and Health Weekly # 697*, May 18,2000, pg. 1

139. Booth, Leo, Father, *When God Becomes A Drug*, (Tarcher/Putnam 1991), pg. 35

140. Booth, pp. 31-32

141. Booth, pp. 31-32

142. Booth, pp. 31-32

143. Booth, pp. 35

144. Miller, Kenneth, R., *Finding Darwin's God: A Scientists Search for Common Ground Between God and Evolution*, (Cliff Street Books-Harper Collins, 1999), pg. 16

145. Fromm, Eric, *The Dogma of Christ*, (Henry Holt, 1963; Owl Book, 1992) pp. 27-28

146. Fromm, pg. 41

147. Fromm, pp. 58-61

148. Heschel, A.J., *Man is Not Alone*, pg. 257

149. Caroll, James, *Constantine's Sword The Church and the Jews: A History* (Houghtlin Mifflin Company, 2001), pg. 200

150. Caroll, pg. 210

151. Caroll, pg. 210

152. Nakken, Craig, *The Addictive Personality*, (Hazelden Foundation, 1996) pg. 29

153. Walsch, Neale Donald, *Conversations with God*an uncommon dialogue*book 1*, (Putnam, 1996) pg. 67

154. Emerson, Ralph Waldo, *Self-Reliance and other Essays*, (Dover Publications, 1993) pg. 83

155. Levoy, Gregg, *Callings, Finding and Following and Authentic Life,* (Three Rivers Press, paperback ed. 1998), pg. 49

0-595-25348-2

www.ingramcontent.com/pod-product-compliance
Lightning Source LLC
Chambersburg PA
CBHW021559280526
45784CB00001BA/414